Pelican Books
Who Cares About Eng...

David Crystal was born in Lisburn, ..., in 1941.
He went to St Mary's College, Liverp..... ...rsity College,
London, where he read English and obtained his Ph.D. in 1966.
He became lecturer in linguistics at University College, Bangor;
and since 1965 has been at the University of Reading, where
he is now Professor. He has been a visiting lecturer in many
parts of Europe, the United States, Canada, Australia, and
South America. His early research was mainly in English
linguistics, particularly intonation and stylistics; his current
research is in the clinical and remedial applications of linguistics
in the study of speech and hearing disorders. He is also interested
in developing the relationship between linguistics and language
teaching in schools.

David Crystal has published numerous articles and reviews, and
is the author of *Linguistics, Language and Religion, What is
Linguistics?, Prosodic Systems and Intonation in English, Linguistics*
(also published by Penguins), *The English Tone of Voice, Child
Language, Learning and Linguistics, Working with LARSP,
Introduction to Language Pathology, A First Dictionary of Linguistics
and Phonetics, Clinical Linguistics, Directions in Applied Linguistics*
and *Profiling Linguistic Disability*, co-author of *Systems of Prosodic
and Paralinguistic Features in English, Investigating English Style,
The English Language, Advanced Conversational English, The
Grammatical Analysis of Language Disability, Skylarks* (a language
development programme) and *Databank* (remedial reading series)
and the editor of *Eric Partridge: In His Own Words* and
Linguistic Controversies. He is a frequent radio broadcaster on
language and linguistics.

David Crystal

Who Cares About English Usage?

Penguin Books

Penguin Books Ltd, Harmondsworth, Middlesex, England
Penguin Books, 40 West 23rd Street, New York, New York 10010, U.S.A.
Penguin Books Australia Ltd, Ringwood, Victoria, Australia
Penguin Books Canada Ltd, 2801 John Street, Markham, Ontario, Canada L3R 1B4
Penguin Books (N.Z.) Ltd, 182–190 Wairau Road, Auckland 10, New Zealand

First published 1984

The cartoons on pp. 23, 35, 56, 81, 94, 103
are reproduced by kind permission of *Punch*.

Made and printed in Great Britain by
Richard Clay (The Chaucer Press) Ltd,
Bungay, Suffolk
Set in Monophoto Photina by
Northumberland Press Ltd, Gateshead

Contents

Introduction

People ask questions about the English language in all kinds of situations. Here are some of them, purloined from recent conversations and correspondence. They ought to be familiar. You've probably been asked a question along these lines in the past few weeks. Maybe you asked one of them yourself. At the very least, it's a safe bet that some of them have crossed your mind.

Child: Why is *bum* rude?
Mother: It just is! You're not to say it!

Tom: How do you pronounce d-i-s-p-u-t-e? Is it 'dis*pute*' or '*dis*pute'?
Harry: 'Dis*pute*' is the proper way – I think.

Son: Dad, I've got to underline the prepositions in this homework. What's a preposition?
Dad: Er, I don't think we did prepositions when I went to school.

Wife (*reading paper*): It says here that Mr Schulz has a 'laid-back' manner. What does 'laid-back' mean?
Husband: I dunno. Look it up in the dictionary.
Wife (*five minutes later*): It isn't in the dictionary.

Railway passenger (*as train goes through Maidenhead*): I wonder what they called it that for? Silly name!
Companion: Oh, I don't know. I think it sounds rather nice, actually.

Anne (*pauses while writing letter*): Is *stationary* spelled with an *A* or an *E*?
Mary: I don't know. I always get them muddled up. Do you mean 'letters' or 'stopped'?
Anne: 'Letters'.
Mary: *A*, I think. I'd be on the safe side. Look it up.

Mrs O: I shall be meeting a Bishop at this evening's dinner. What do I call him?

Mr O: Why not just 'Bishop'?
Mrs O: That sounds a bit brusque. Isn't it supposed to be 'My Lord'?
Mr O: I don't like that. Sounds as if you're in church!

Dear Sir,

I am appalled at the way standards of English are deteriorating these days. Can't you do something about it?

Wife: I wonder what's the origin of 'A rolling stone gathers no moss'?
Husband: Well, whatever it was, I bet it wasn't Mick Jagger!

Son: Dad, do I put a semi-colon or a colon here in this sentence?
Dad: Ask your mother.

Wife (*playing Scrabble*): There! F,I,C,H,U.
Husband: There's no such word, is there?
Wife: 'Course there is! It's a sort of shawl.
Husband: Never! You're making it up.
Wife: Let's look it up, then ... (*looks in dictionary*) ... There!

Mike (*watching TV news*): Did you hear that? They say the terrorists have 'claimed' responsibility for that attack – as if it was something to be proud of! There must be a better word, mustn't there?
Fred (*thinks*): Perhaps 'admit' would be better?
Mike: Anything would be better than 'claimed', I think.
Fred: Why don't you write and tell them.
Mike: Tell who? The terrorists?
Fred: No, dummy! The BBC – whoever writes the news.

Daughter: Mum, I've finished my application letter. How do I end it? Yours faithfully?
Mum: Depends how you started it.

Dear Sir,

Will you please, please do something about the falling standards of spoken English on the radio and TV these days? Yesterday I heard three split infinitives in as many minutes!

Wife (*writing up minutes of a meeting*): Do I put 'The committee is' or 'The committee are'?
Husband: Both sound all right to me.
Wife: That's no help!

Child: I've finished my draw-r-ing.

Mother: Don't say 'draw-r-ing', darling. It's 'draw-ing', isn't it.

Child: Draw-ing. I've finished my draw-r-ing now.

Husband (*reading paper*): Look at this! They're advertising for a 'sales-person' now. Why can't they say 'salesman'! Sometimes I think this equal sex business is going a bit far.

Wife: No it's not. It's very sensible. *I* couldn't apply if it were 'sales-man'.

Husband: I still think 'salesman and saleswoman' would be better.

Mr X: Which is it? *I will* or *I shall*?

Mr Y: Which is it? *Disinterested* or *uninterested*?

Mr Z: Which is it? *Different to* or *different from*?

Some of these questions are easy to answer. If you aren't sure of the spelling difference between *stationary* and *stationery*, for instance, all you have to do is look it up. There are no problems – apart from remembering the difference for next time. Standard English usage is united on this one.

On the other hand, some of the questions are not so easy. A new word, like 'laid-back', may take years before it turns up in a dictionary – so how do you check on its meaning before then? Finding out about the origins and history of words (their 'etymology') is a complicated piece of historical detective work, not always successful, in view of the distance in time you often have to travel.

Most questions about modern English usage have more than one answer. Does everyone find *bum* equally rude? Is splitting an infinitive really such a crime? Can there be more than one correct pronunciation for a word?

This book is about the linguistic problem cases. I've selected some of the awkward or difficult questions which are always being raised about usage – whether on radio or television, in the press, or just in everyday conversation. I know these questions are asked, because in recent years I've found myself having to answer them, partly in teaching students and foreign learners, but mainly in relation to my radio programmes on language, such as *Speak Out*. Some of them have been discussed in English books for nearly two hundred years. Others are the product of the twentieth-century communications explosion.

My experience is that people fall into three broad groups, in their concern over how their language works. Some couldn't care less. Many

– I think, the majority – care at least some of the time. And some care all of the time. I have tried to write a book which will be of interest to all three groups. I hope it will be useful to you, whether you are a member of the first group, and have never even dreamed about English usage; or a member of the second, who have lost only the occasional wink of sleep over it; or a member of the third, who regularly have nightmares about it. Readers from all three groups should at least find the topics familiar. After all, it was you who asked the questions, provided many of the illustrations, and gave all the answers. It's *your* usage in these pages, not mine.

But you can't really care about something, or take care of it properly, until you come to know it. So this book has a serious, underlying purpose, beneath the cartoons – to inform and advise about English usage. I am a firm believer in the need to talk about the language clearly and accurately, so that problems of communication can be identified and solved. But I am totally against any approach which over-intellectualizes the subject, or pontificates without reason, as has happened so often in the past. Something has gone seriously wrong, when so many people find themselves looking back at their English grammar lessons at school, remembering only the pain, or boredom, or – nothing. It is perfectly possible to *enjoy* thinking about your language, and trying to analyse it – as evidenced by the success of such programmes as *Call My Bluff* and *Blankety Blank*. I thoroughly enjoy finding out about English, whether in a research library or in the street, and it is this, above all, which I've tried to get across in the sometimes light-hearted discussions on questions of usage.

Most of these questions don't have simple answers in terms of Right *vs* Wrong, or Correct *vs* Incorrect. This is what makes them interesting, of course. When we investigate them, and the reasons why people talk and worry about them, we find ourselves in a fascinating world of truths and half-truths, public and private attitudes, and fiercely held differences of opinion. It's an emotional world, full of feelings of linguistic pride, envy, anger, sloth – indeed, most of the seven deadly sins seem to have their language equivalents. It's a sensitive world, too, with feelings that can be quickly bruised, linguistic toes that can be easily stepped on, linguistic bricks that can be readily dropped. It's a world where sticks and stones break bones, and names hurt as well.

Language doesn't exist in a vacuum. It reflects all the life and variety and change and divisions which exist in society. If there are few simple answers to the language questions in this book, it's because the social situations they relate to are themselves complex. The study of our language opens all kinds of doors – into our own personalities and backgrounds, and into the lives of those with whom we interact. To understand and appreciate someone else's use of language is a major step along the road to understanding them as people. To fail to understand or appreciate their language erects a social and psychological barrier immediately. They don't talk like us. They aren't like us. Maybe they don't like us ...

There will always be social division, and so there will always be linguistic variety. We can't remove this variety, but we can learn about it, and try to understand the way it shapes our attitudes and outlook. At the very least, it's a pleasant enough way to pass the time. At best, some good might come out of the enterprise, in the form of greater linguistic – and therefore social – tolerance. It's no coincidence that 'communication' and 'community' are closely related words.

You know *you know* ... ?

There's nothing that irritates me more than having to listen to some empty-headed person being interviewed on radio and TV, when he's asked a perfectly straightforward question, and he pads out his answer with a flood of *you knows*.

So wrote one angry radio listener. Nor is it just *you know* which is singled out for attack. There are several words and phrases which people insert into their speech, and which attract criticism when they are over-used. Some of them can be seen in the following conversation – which isn't entirely fictitious:

> Interviewer: So why has your policy changed?
> Famous Person: Well, you know, there hasn't been, you know, a change, as it were, in the usual sense of that word ... you see, I mean, there is in fact a difference between change and, you know, development, so to say ...

No one would be happy with this kind of reply – especially if it came from somebody whose standing might lead you to expect something rather more confident and coherent.

That's why many people object to *you know*, *you see*, *mind you*, *I mean*, and all the other 'parenthetic' phrases of this kind. They are held to be signs of unclear thinking, or lack of confidence, and anyone anxious to develop a controlled, precise speech style, or an authoritative public image, would do well to avoid them. Some people go further. In their view, phrases like *you know* should be scrupulously eradicated from the language in the next major clean-up exercise. They are of no value. They communicate no meaning. So let's get rid of them. Enough said?

No. There's far more to be said about these little phrases. They *do* have a job to do in modern English. They *do* communicate meaning – though it's often a different kind of meaning than many people expect. To get rid of them entirely would be a real loss, not a gain, for the language.

To see this, let's look again at the Famous Person interview, and ask what was wrong with it. Two things. There were too many *you know*-type phrases. And they were being used in a situation where clear and precise thinking was expected. The Famous Person might have got away with just one or two of these phrases – but to use ten of them in his opening couple of sentences was positively foolhardy.

But now reflect on a quite different situation, where clear and precise thinking is *not* the order of the day, and where there is no public image to be concerned about. At home, out shopping, in the pub, in a canteen ... in innumerable everyday settings where there is no external pressure on us to speak according to a national standard, where no one is listening to us in order to judge us, or our fluency, and where people use language just as a form of social cement, to chat rather than to converse – in these domestic settings, conversation operates with a very different set of linguistic standards from those we try to use in formal situations. And one of the most important differences is the use we make of such phrases as *you know* – introducing them into our speech in such a natural and unselfconscious way that neither speaker nor listener becomes aware of the fact that they've been used at all.

Here's an example, with *you know* turning up at the beginning of a sentence:

Claude: Any more tins left in the cupboard?
Arthur: Can't see any.
Claude: Y'know, I think it's about time we went shopping.

The phrase is said quickly, with the *you* often shortened to a rapidly pronounced *y'*. This is a very frequent usage in informal conversation. You can see what job it does by putting two sentences side by side, the only difference being the use of *you know* at the beginning of one of them. I'll illustrate from a 'telling-off' context. First, the *you know*-less version:

Father (*to erring daughter*): You really must be in before 11.30.

This sounds abrupt, serious, no negotiations. Here's the alternative.

Father: Y'know, you really must be in before 11.30.

This sounds much less abrupt. The force of the telling-off is softened. There's a hint of sympathy – we all know life is hard, but ... I wouldn't be at all surprised to see a paternal arm around the shoulders, accompanying the second example. And if I were the teenage daughter in question, I might well have a go at getting round him.

The same 'softening' effect can also be heard when *y'know* turns up in the middle or at the end of a sentence. Father might have said:

You really must be in by 11.30, y'know.

And Claude might have said:

I think, y'know, it's about time we went shopping.

But beware! If you put more than one *y'know* into the same sentence, you don't just get a straightforward increase in softening power. The sentence begins to sound weird:

Y'know, you really must be in by 11.30, y'know.

or pathologically non-fluent:

Y'know, I think, y'know, it's about time, y'know, we went shopping y'know.

Here's a different use of *you know* at the beginning of a sentence:

Claude: I can't find that book.
Arthur: Which one?
Claude: You know, the one I was reading last night.

This time, the *you know* is said more slowly, with the *you* given a full pronunciation. Here it has more of a literal meaning: 'You will be the one who knows – if you think about what I'm just about to say.' It can even be used on its own:

Arthur: Which one?
Claude: You know!
Arthur: Oh yes, the new one.

or, of course, alternatively:

Arthur: No, I don't know. You read so many these days.

As before, this use of *you know* can be found in the middle or at the end of a sentence. Claude in due course might say:

I'll just pop down to the shop – you know, the one on the corner.

Here, the *you know* helps to sort out an ambiguity: what follows it is the information that Arthur needs to be sure of Claude's meaning.

At the end of a sentence, the phrase can add various meanings. It can act as a check on the listener's understanding, for instance. Claude might say:

> I saw a pair of those red, fur-lined earphones in the hi-fi shop, you
>   know?

Here, the phrase is used to mean 'Are you with me?', 'Do you know what I mean?'. In this use, it was a common tag in hippie talk a few years ago.

> That's real cool, man, you know?

Also, at the end of a sentence, the phrase can add a conspiratorial nuance, especially said low down in the voice:

> I just saw Myrtle Jones in the street with – you know!

If you don't know, you'll be keen to find out.

Sometimes, far from expressing imprecision, *you know* expresses a very precise nuance indeed. Take the following neutral remark made by someone at a party:

> James and his friend have just arrived.

Adding *you know* can alter the meaning quite dramatically:

> James and his, you know, friend have just arrived.

The phrase focuses our attention on the following word, and suggests that there's something special about its meaning. Of course, if the following word is one where no special sense could be involved, the use of *you know* would be highly unlikely. For instance, to obtain a plausible special meaning which would allow

> James and his, you know, budgie have just arrived

you have to engage in some quite ingenious mental manoeuvres.

Lastly, it's worth noting that *you know*, and the other phrases of this kind, are governed by rules of English grammar, just like any other piece of sentence construction. You can't put a *you know* into any sort of sentence, and assume that the result will sound like normal conversational English. All the sentences used so far, for instance, are of the kind grammar books refer to as 'statements'. *You know*s are much rarer with other types of sentence, and it's not difficult to think up sentences where the use of *you know* would sound quite bizarre.

You'd be unlikely to use this phrase to precede a question, say:

> You know, is it six o'clock?
> You know, has your mother arrived?

Or a command:

> You know, shut the door!
> You know, pass the salt, please!

Or an exclamation. Would you bang your thumb with a hammer and then say:

> You know, damn!

Or try this. See in how many places you could plausibly insert a *you know* in the following sentence. You certainly won't be able to have the phrase between every pair of words, and still have natural English. There's a space to mark whether you find the sentence acceptable or not.

> Between you and me, John does not want to travel to New York next week.

Acceptable *Unacceptable*

Between, you know, you and me, John does not want to travel to New York next week.

Between you, you know, and me, John does not want to travel to New York next week.

Between you and, you know, me, John does not want to travel to New York next week.

Between you and me, you know, John does not want to travel to New York next week.

Between you and me, John, you know, does not want to travel to New York next week.

Between you and me, John does, you know, not want to travel to New York next week.

Between you and me, John does not, you know, want to travel to New York next week.

Between you and me, John does not want, you know, to travel to New York next week.

Between you and me, John does not want to, you know, travel to New York next week.

Between you and me, John does not want to travel, you know, to New York next week.

Between you and me, John does not want to travel to, you know, New York next week.

Between you and me, John does not want to travel to New, you know, York next week.

Between you and me, John does not want to travel to New York, you know, next week.

Between you and me, John does not want to travel to New York next, you know, week.

This whole section has been about just one of the little phrases which have attracted so much criticism. And of course, if they are *over*-used, the criticism is justified. Over-using *any* bit of language arouses irritation in a listener or reader. Even a harmless word like *really* begins to irritate if people really start to use the word really unnecessarily, and where there is really no special reason, such as a really poetic effect that they are really trying to obtain! When *you know* is over-used, it draws attention to itself, and gets in the way of communication. But in moderation, it can be a valuable tool for the expression of subtle nuances and stylistic effects.

There must be hundreds of these parenthetic phrases in modern spoken English. I like to think of them as the oil which helps speech to run smoothly. Listen out for them, and you'll quickly draw up a lengthy list, many of which will be used in written English too. Here are some, culled from conversations I've heard recently. The rest of the next page is free for you to add further items you may have noticed yourselves.

... as a matter of fact ...   ... the trouble is ...
... mind you ...   ... to put it another way ...
... you see ...   ... what's more ...

... speaking as a laymen ...   ... as you say ...
... off the record ...   ... I suppose ...
... what annoys me ...   ... sort of ...
... God knows ...

S.O.S. *1. It's only* only

S.O.S., as everyone knows, stands for 'Save Our Syntax'. At various places in this book, I'll be discussing under this heading a grammatical point which regularly causes people to send up distress rockets, and demand linguistic lifejackets.

Where should the little adverb *only* be placed in a sentence? A simple question, but a frequent cause of raised blood pressure.

In everyday conversational English, you'll usually hear sentences like these:

He only died last week.   I've only got six sweets.
I only saw Fred, not Jim.   They only arrived at 2.

All perfectly natural and idiomatic.

But for as long as people have been writing books on English grammar and usage, sentences like these have been castigated. If you put *only* before the verb, in these sentences, you allow ambiguity – or so it is argued. The critics say: Take a sentence like *I only saw Fred.* Does this mean

'I only saw Fred – and not someone else'

or

'I only saw Fred – I didn't speak to him'?

You can't tell, just by looking at the sentence, they say. It's ambiguous. But there wouldn't be any ambiguity if *only* were put next to the word whose meaning it limits. Compare:

I saw only Fred   and   I only saw Fred.

If everyone followed this rule, there'd never be any trouble. Hence, the critics conclude, sentences such as those cited above should be altered. They should be:

He died only last week.   I've got only six sweets.
I saw only Fred, not Jim.   They arrived only at 2.

Some people get very upset about this issue. They attempt always to speak and write their *only*s according to the 'good neighbours' rule, and they're quick to criticize others when they spot them misplacing an *only*. Some correspondents admit to keeping a special eye open for *only* errors. Sir Ernest Gowers, in his book on usage, *Plain Words*, went so far as to talk about the popular sport of '*only*-snooping'.

But if the sport is popular, so is the usage. You can trace it back to the fifteenth century, in fact, and you'll find it in most authors. Two lines from a Shakespeare sonnet (No. 94) will perhaps be enough to indicate its honourable ancestry:

> The summer's flower is to the summer sweet
> Though to itself it only live and die . . .

And these days, it's perfectly normal in conversational English.

Can the argument be resolved? Yes – but only if you keep two principles in mind. First, the way speech works is different from the way writing works. Where you put *only* may at times lead to ambiguous written language, but it never causes problems in speech, because the way in which you say the sentence sorts out which word goes with which. Listen to this sentence said three ways. The word in heavy type is said loudest. After each sentence, I'll add a gloss to show its interpretation:

> I only told him **yesterday** – he hasn't had time to think about it yet.
> I only told **him** yesterday – I didn't tell his friends.
> I only **told** him yesterday – I didn't hit him or anything.

The rule in speech is simple: *only* goes with the word which is loudest. There isn't any ambiguity.

But this argument can't work for the written language, where loudness doesn't exist. So here you have to bear in mind the second principle: a sentence may seem ambiguous by itself, but put it into context, and the ambiguity may disappear. Take the sentence:

> The policeman was ordered to stop drinking on the streets.

On the face of it, wholly ambiguous. Who was doing the drinking? The policeman? or someone else? But this sentence would hardly ever be ambiguous in real life, because the context would make it clear what was meant. Because you know that policemen don't usually drink on the streets, and *are* concerned with law and order, you'd interpret the sentence one way. And often there'd be other sentences around to back up your interpretation, such as:

> The policeman was ordered to stop drinking on the streets.
> He promised he would never do it again.

The same factors affect the use of *only*, in the written language. Is a sentence such as *He only died last week* really ambiguous? Enough to warrant the re-placing of *only*? Is there ever a situation where 'He only died' would be a likely interpretation? Or take *I've only got six sweets*. How likely is it that such a sentence would be misunderstood? Not likely at all, most people would say. Those who insist on re-placing *only* in such sentences are not going to convince others that they have a valid point.

Now, most of the sentences which turn up in *only*-debates are like these. They aren't really ambiguous at all. They only seem so when taken out of context and waved about as an example of an Issue. The pity of it is that all this *only*-waving can obscure the existence of the few genuine cases of ambiguity that could be cited. If you are an *only*-snooper, you will be rewarded, every now and again, by a real case of ambiguity, where you can't tell from the context what the sentence means. Here's an example:

> The situation will only be alleviated by an immediate pay-offer.

The context was an industrial dispute. The sentence came from a newspaper report. But it was quite unclear from the adjoining sentences whether the writer meant:

> (i) The pay-offer will only alleviate the situation, not solve it,

or

> (ii) Only a pay-offer will alleviate the situation, nothing else.

So, it *is* important to be cautious about the place of *only*, in the written language. It can cause problems. But it doesn't very often. When it does, there are grounds for complaint, for the writer has not been clear. But there are no grounds, in my view, for blood pressure to go up *every* time an *only* is sighted. There are better causes to fight for.

*

In fact, *only* isn't the only word which limits the meaning of another word in the same sentence. Here are some other common 'limiting' or 'focusing' words, which do the same kind of job, and raise the same kind of problem. There's a place to mark your preference; and then, listen out, to see whether you're in the majority.

	Version A	Version B	Your preference	Other people's preference
also	I also saw John at the party.	I saw also John at the party.	A B	A B
just	I just ate the peas, not the potatoes.	I ate just the peas, not the potatoes.	A B	A B
merely	I merely wanted to know.	I wanted merely to know.	A B	A B
simply	I simply had to leave.	I had simply to leave.	A B	A B
even	I even asked Mary to go with me.	I asked even Mary to go with me.	A B	A B
mainly	I mainly travelled by car.	I travelled mainly by car.	A B	A B

You might also like to note down any cases of *only* which strike you as *really* ambiguous, as you read and listen, as a reminder of possible pitfalls. But remember to check the context for clues first.

'Isn't there a stronger word than Guilty?'

To boldly split, or not to split?

I am now talking about infinitives, not atoms or personalities. The 'split infinitive' has been an arch-enemy of those who wish to establish a kingdom of pure English grammar here on earth. It is one of the most hated 'errors' of usage. Letter-writers say such things as:

> Listening to the eight o'clock news on the wireless this morning, I was appalled to hear that two infinitives had been split within three minutes of each other.

It is also one of the most talked-about topics in books on the subject. So we had better be clear about what infinitives are, in the first place.

'Infinitive' is the term grammarians use to talk about verbs in their most naked state – seen without the endings and other changes which are so frequently used, when verbs turn up in language. Take a verb like *take*. It adds endings: *He takes, He's taking, He was taken*. It can also change its shape: *He took*. Young children who are trying to master its irregular grammar make up other forms – I've heard them say *tooken, tooked* and *taked*, as they try to sort things out. I've heard foreigners say *They were takings* and *He was takened*.

But what would you say, if some foreigner were to ask you:

> Please, what is *took*? What does it mean?

If you knew some grammar, you'd probably say something like:

> It's the past tense form of the verb *take*.

But what if you didn't know any grammatical terminology? You'd still be able to answer, for after all, as a mother-tongue speaker of English you *do know* (though you may not be very used to talking about what you know). One person I asked, who professed to knowing no grammar at all, said:

> Well, it's like *take* – only *took* is for saying that it's happened already, and *take* is happening now.

That's not bad at all.

The point to notice is that both these answers find it necessary to refer to *take*, in order to explain the other form. And actually, whichever form of the verb you might be asked to explain, you'd always find this happening. What is *taking*? That's easy: it's the verb *take* with an *-ing* ending (plus the nuisance of a change in the spelling). What is *takes*? *Take* + *-s*.

All verbs have a basic form, as with *take*, and this is the one you cite when you want to talk about 'the verb'. It's also the one you'd always find as the head-word in a dictionary. You would look up *take*, if you wanted to find something out about this verb's meaning. You wouldn't expect all the information to be listed under *taken* or *took*. (Not in English, anyway. Not all languages organize their dictionaries like this. Arabic doesn't, for instance.)

This basic form of the verb is called the *infinitive*.

So what is split? The word *take* itself? No. There doesn't seem to be any occasion in English when speakers split this word into two, and put another word in between. You've never heard:

> I'm going to ta-quickly-ke the book back.

The same applies to other verbs. Words don't get split up like this, in a language like English. For there to be a 'split infinitive', there have to be at least two words.

The other word is *to*. When infinitives are used in English sentences, they are very often preceded by *to*. For instance:

> Fred: Do you want *to dance*?
> Suzanne: No, thanks. I'd prefer *to sit* this one out.

Or, if you would rather have literary examples:

> *To be* or not *to be* ...

> *To err* is human, *to forgive* divine ...

In cases like this, you can't leave the *to* out. Only a foreigner, a young child, or someone with a language disorder would say:

> Do you want dance?

When people talk about the 'split infinitive', they are referring to sentences where another word has been put between *to* and the verb.

This sort of thing:

> I want *to* quickly *run* up to Boots to pick up my prescription.
> Have you asked him *to* not *have* his radio on so loud?
> He's hoping *to* really *get* his teeth into it.

I suppose the most widely known split infinitive, this side of the twenty-third century, is:

> *To* boldly *go* where no man has gone before!

which was used as part of the introduction to the TV series *Star Trek*. It led to the following remark, which has nowadays become a cliché in its own right:

> To boldly split infinitives, where none were split before.

Split infinitives are extremely common in everyday conversation and in informal writing (letters and postcards, for instance), which tends to follow the rhythms of speech. You'll hear them a lot on radio and television, especially in plays, sitcoms, and all forms of unscripted discussion. You won't hear them a great deal in formal broadcast speech, however – announcers, newscasters, programme presenters and others are generally anxious to avoid such things, because they are all too aware of the complaints which will come if they let one slip into their speech – witness the ferocious tone of the letter at the beginning of this section.

But why should people get so upset about whether *to* is separated from its verb? There's no doubt that many people feel very strongly about it. I've had correspondence in which splitting the infinitive is referred to as a degradation, a corruption, a cheapening, a mutilation of the language. It's been called clumsy, ugly, awkward, tasteless, graceless, barbarous, vulgar, odious and loathsome!

I can't help thinking this is going a bit far, especially as most of the well-known writers in English literature have all split their infinitives at various points in their work. The list of splitters dates back to the fourteenth century, and includes such names as John Wycliffe, John Donne, Samuel Taylor Coleridge, Oliver Goldsmith and George Eliot. A couple of examples:

> ... without permitting himself to actually mention the name ...

(wrote Matthew Arnold)

... as he happens to newly consider it ...

(wrote Robert Browning).
One irate radio listener wrote:

> I always think of Lord Macaulay as a paragon of style. I am sure
> he would never have split an infinitive.

In fact, he did. He even deliberately changed his word order, when he
was revising an article for publication in 1843, preferring the split form.
Instead of

> in order fully to appreciate

he wrote

> in order to fully appreciate.

So there can't be anything *inherently* ugly in the split infinitive, if
so many excellent writers have used it. Nor can the language be getting
corrupted *now*, if the practice has been around since the fourteenth
century, at least. Where, then, does the upset come from?

In my view, the explanation has two parts. In part one, we have to
go back to school. For many people, strong feelings about the English
language stem from the way they were taught about it in school. One
correspondent was quite clear why *he* got worked up about split infinitives:
he didn't want to waste his suffering! He wrote:

> The reason why the older generation feel so strongly about English
> grammar is that we were severely punished if we didn't obey the
> rules! One split infinitive, one whack; two split infinitives, two
> whacks; and so on.

Whether whacked or not, I can indeed understand the feelings of those
people who may have worked through hours of grammar exercises, on
these points. The homework, as well as the cane, will have left its mark,
and helped to shape the style of many thousands of speakers and writers
of English.

But this is only part one of the explanation. For we must now ask:
Why did everyone get taught about split infinitives at school in the first
place? Whose idea was that?

The short answer is: It was the idea of the grammar-book authors
who were writing in the early nineteenth century. There's hardly any

mention of the split infinitive in the books on English written by eighteenth-century authors. The fuss has been with us for less than two hundred years.

The grammarians' reasoning probably went something like this. 'One of the most beautiful languages ever used by man was Latin. Look at its magnificent literature! Look at the wonderful style of authors like Cicero! English would do very well if it could live up to the standards of a language like Latin.'

Many pieces of English grammar came to be shaped along the lines of Latin grammar, at that time. The idea of the infinitive, amongst others. To see how, you first have to know that phrases like *to run*, *to jump*, *to love* – two words in English – would in Latin be translated by a single word. *To love* in Latin is *amare*. The reasoning was simple: you can't split *amare*, and the other infinitives, in Latin – so you shouldn't split *to love*, and the other infinitives, in English!

It's only recently that people have begun to criticize the view that English ought to be shaped to fit the rules of Latin. These days, the fashion is to study a language as it is. Latin is no longer a dominant influence in education, though that is a source of regret to many. Indeed, it's hardly ever taught in schools, now.

But a hundred years ago, you couldn't be thought of as educated without a knowledge of Latin. And, amongst other things, this meant showing in your English speech and writing that you 'knew the rules'. To split the infinitive became one of the signs of a lack of education, or of carelessness. And, as we have seen, they had ways of making people talk properly, in those days.

The fuss about the split infinitive is probably beginning to die out, nowadays. New generations of adults have gone through school without ever having heard of a split infinitive. When I first talked about this issue on the radio, several younger listeners wrote to me asking what the fuss was about? They'd never come across it before. The new ways of teaching the English language in schools don't look at grammar in the same way as a hundred years ago.

But the worries and fears about splitting the infinitive haven't died out yet. Indeed, they're very much alive in the memories of the older generations, who in turn transmit their fears to those of the younger generations anxious not to put a linguistic foot wrong. It takes only one intolerant boss to correct a junior's letter for the old world to return. We don't usually whack with canes any more, but we do with words.

Take this conversation, for instance, extracted from the middle of a long argument about the existence of God:

> Jim (*very defensively*): ... so I don't see why anyone should accept that kind of rubbishy remark.
>
> Michael (*pressing point home*): But if you want to really get an insight into it, you –
>
> Jim (*interrupting*): What sort of language is that?
>
> Michael: Eh?
>
> Jim: 'To really get'. That's typical of the careless way you people put things. If you aren't going to use proper grammar, I don't see why we should take your sort of view seriously ...

And so on. Not a very relevant remark, but a good ploy for putting someone off his stride. If you can't use sticks or stones to break mental bones, try names – or, even better, grammatical constructions.

There's another reason why many people are more tolerant about split infinitives these days than was once the case. Twentieth-century studies of English speech and writing have brought to light many cases where the split infinitive has a *useful* role to play. It can help to avoid an ambiguity, for instance. Here are three conversations. A similar sentence turns up in the middle of each, but the word *deliberately* changes its position each time. Notice how the meaning changes.

> 1. Fred: We've often found ourselves having a row, and realized the kids are in the room, listening –
> Mary: So we've tried to deliberately stop arguing –
> Fred: But it isn't easy ...

Here, it's the stopping which is deliberate.

> 2. Fred: ... and I said *I* could stop arguing if *she* could.
> Mary: So I tried deliberately – to stop arguing for a while, just to see ...

Here, it's Mary's trying which is deliberate.

> 3. Fred: I don't mind rows when there's a reason, but sometimes you seem to want to start one off on purpose.
> Mary: But I have *tried* to stop arguing deliberately like that ...

Here, it's Mary's arguing which is deliberate.

There are other cases, too, where allowing the split infinitive is useful, because it leads to a more natural rhythm of speech. Which do you find the most natural of the following sentences?

> He was trying   to definitely hold the ball.
>   definitely to hold the ball.
>   to hold definitely the ball.

Not the third, presumably, which sounds a bit like a foreigner speaking. If you were brought up on split infinitives, you will be conscience-bound to opt for the second. But if you try this exercise out on people who haven't had any training in grammar, and who are just using their 'feel' for the language in order to judge, you will find that the vast majority prefer the first.

That's why the *Star Trek* usage was so effective, of course. *To boldly go* has one big thing in its favour. It is following the natural rhythm of English – the te-tum te-tum rhythm favoured by Shakespeare and which is the mainstay of our poetic tradition. If the scriptwriter had written *boldly to go*, the two weak syllables would have come together, and this would have sounded jerky. If he had written *to go boldly*, he would have ended up with two strong syllables together, which sounds ponderous. *To boldly go* is rhythmically very neat. The *Star Trek* script-writer hasn't really been linguistically bold at all.

So – if you find yourself using a split infinitive, I certainly don't believe that you ought to feel conscience-stricken, and start imagining that you are one of those who are helping to corrupt the English language. And faced with someone else using a split infinitive, I wouldn't immediately point out his 'error', or write to the BBC and complain about falling standards. Remember Lord Macaulay, and the others.

On the other hand, once you know that this is a sensitive area of English usage, it would be sensible to be cautious. There's more chance of you upsetting someone if you do use a split infinitive than if you don't. If I were addressing a public audience – giving a formal speech, or a radio talk, for instance – I would know that there could well be people in the audience who would be upset, or get distracted, if I used one – so I would go out of my way not to do so. I don't want my listeners distracted by my grammar, when I'm trying to get them to follow my meaning. The same applies when I am writing for public consumption. I would use a split infinitive only when the meaning or rhythm really justified it. I wouldn't put them in just for the sake of it. I'd rather judge each case on its merits.

*

On the rest of this page, there's a space for you to check your own preferences about split infinitives. I've listed a few cases that I've heard or seen recently. There's a space for you to tick whether you'd accept it or correct it, and another space to write in your alternative phrasing. At the bottom and on the next page, there's room to add any further examples you've come across yourself.

	Acceptable	*Unacceptable*	*Alternative?*
I want to actually see you in the view-finder.			
I don't want you to so much as speak to her.			
I want you to seriously consider your position.			
I want you to really try.			
Do you want to further prolong this debate?			

Which is it? Round 1

There are a remarkable number of words in standard English that are very easy to confuse. Some pairs of words are pronounced the same, but spelt differently. Others are quite different in pronunciation and spelling, but very similar in meaning. If you want to produce acceptable, standard English, you've got to get the distinctions right. You have to choose the right word for the right context. Get it wrong, and there's no salvation from anyone. Not even me.

These problems are not like most of the topics discussed elsewhere in this book. Usually, when people complain about usage, or ask 'Which is correct?' I take the line – 'Well, it depends ...'. When some educated people say one thing, and others say another, there's room for debate. You could write a book about the issues involved. But the four 'rounds' of 'Which is it?' questions in this book illustrate confusions which are of a different kind. Here, there's no disagreement amongst educated people over what is correct. Here, Right and Wrong rule. O.K.?

So, if you make a mistake in one of the following sentences, it is very definitely a Mistake, from the point of view of standard English. But it's important to put the error in perspective. Some mistakes are serious, in that you end up saying or writing something quite different from what you intended. But others are not too serious, in that it may be perfectly clear from the context what you meant. Sometimes, even, the mistake won't be noticed – especially in the rush of conversation. Occasionally – *very* occasionally – mistakes of this kind become quite widespread, start being used by influential people, creep into the written language, and in due course become standard usage – by which time, of course, people would have stopped regarding them as mistakes. But usually, it is the influential people themselves who notice the mistake first, and condemn it. There has certainly been plenty of condemnation heaped on the heads of those who confuse the eighty words listed in the four rounds of 'Which is it?'

The problem cases are presented in the form of a quiz. Each item illustrates a common confusion. There's a sample sentence, with the alternatives provided. Alongside each sentence, there's a space to write in the form which you think is correct. If you need to, you can go to page 120 for the answers, and for some discussion of any interesting points of usage. There are no prizes for getting them all right. And no sanctions for getting them all wrong. But for comparison, you might like to know that I tried the questions out on twenty English undergraduates, and got scores ranging from 25 to 40.

1. Shall we $\begin{Bmatrix} \text{accept} \\ \text{except} \end{Bmatrix}$ his invitation to dinner? _____

2. His words $\begin{Bmatrix} \text{affected} \\ \text{effected} \end{Bmatrix}$ me greatly. _____

3. He's under no $\begin{Bmatrix} \text{allusions} \\ \text{illusions} \end{Bmatrix}$ about the dangers. _____

4. In later life, he $\begin{Bmatrix} \text{amended} \\ \text{emended} \end{Bmatrix}$ his ways. _____

5. Can you $\begin{Bmatrix} \text{assure} \\ \text{insure} \\ \text{ensure} \end{Bmatrix}$ that the dog won't escape? _____

6. I was completely $\begin{Bmatrix} \text{bereft} \\ \text{bereaved} \end{Bmatrix}$ of ideas. _____

7. It's a $\begin{Bmatrix} \text{biannual} \\ \text{biennial} \end{Bmatrix}$ journal, so it'll be out again in six months. _____

8. The chair was $\begin{Bmatrix} \text{born} \\ \text{borne} \end{Bmatrix}$ aloft. _____

9. He was wearing a $\begin{Bmatrix} \text{ceremonial} \\ \text{ceremonious} \end{Bmatrix}$ uniform. _____

10. That's a $\begin{Bmatrix} \text{classic} \\ \text{classical} \end{Bmatrix}$ example of his stupidity! _____

(Solutions are on p. 120)

'I miss the good old days when all we had to worry about was nouns and verbs.'

Should intruders keep out?

Believe it or not, there was once a Society for the Protection of the Letter R. Its members felt that R needed looking after, as it so often led to problems of pronunciation in everyday speech. I don't know if the Society still exists. It may well have gone the way of many such movements, and died a natural death after a few years. R.I.P.

But even if the Society doesn't exist any longer, the problem certainly does. R continues to be one of the most complained about letters, or sounds, in the language. Here is a typical complaint:

> Surely R is the most misused letter in the alphabet? Why oh why do news readers, disc jockeys and speakers of all types put in Rs in words where there are none? Nothing is more irritating to listen to on radio or TV.

Another writer begins:

> Some time ago I ventured to write to one of your best and clearest BBC speakers, to blame him for allowing an 'intrusive r' into his talk. When I (now aged 75) was educated, this was considered a serious mispronunciation. Since receiving his reply, I have been keeping an ear on Radio 4 participants, and have been astonished and – let me admit – horrified at the extreme prevalence of this error among today's talkers. In a couple of hours' listening on Radio 4, I hear maybe 20 intrusives – eight in one *Kaleidoscope* alone!

And here's a third example – though this one is different:

> One of the greatest offenders in this matter is a well-known opposition speaker whom I shall not name. The startling way in which he brings out *idear* is enough to make the hair of anyone but a well-seasoned Cockney stand on end.

The difference is that this was written by Henry Alford, Dean of Canterbury, in his book *The Queen's English*, published in 1869. Intrusive R was evidently around long before the BBC was born, or even conceived!

Why have so many good people been getting so upset about this issue for so long? And why pick on R, anyway?

R needn't be too concerned. The principle that's at stake here affects other letters and sounds as well.

Lots of people say *strength* without the G

complained one correspondent.

What's happened to the L at the end of *school*?

asks another.

Why don't people pronounce the T in *often* more often?
Shouldn't speakers put an F into the phrase *cuppa tea*?
Why isn't there . . .

But there's no need to go on. Most consonants in the alphabet have been charged with offences ranging from loitering with intent to gross indecency. So have they anything to say for themselves? – bearing in mind that their pronunciations will be taken down, phonetically transcribed, and may be used in evidence later.

If I were retained as defence lawyer, the first thing I'd want to do is draw the attention of the jury to the nature of the underlying principle involved. I would point out that the problem arises out of the complex relationships between English sounds and English spellings – the origins of which date back many hundreds of years. As everyone knows who's tried to learn to spell, the relationship between pronunciation and spelling in modern English isn't at all straightforward. There are hundreds of exceptions, which have to be learned off by heart. Remember *dough, ought, through, cough,* and all the others?

But it wasn't always like this. When English speech first came to be written down, just over a thousand years ago, in the form of Anglo-Saxon, the inventors of the alphabet worked very sensibly and logically. When they heard a sound, it was given a letter. No sound, no letter. Same sound, same letter. And when the Latin alphabet which they were using turned out not to have enough letters to cope with the sounds of English, they borrowed letters from other alphabets to cope. There's no TH in Latin, for instance – so they used the appropriate runic symbol, whenever they wanted to write the TH sounds of Anglo-Saxon. The alien appearance of Anglo-Saxon is largely due to these borrowed letters, as in this sort of thing:

þe þillað þið þam ȝolde ȝrið fæstnian

But pronunciation, like the people who do the pronouncing, doesn't stand still. It's affected by social change – and especially by massive cultural developments, such as happened when the Norman French took over. To begin with, English spelling tried to keep pace with the changes in pronunciation. Early Middle English, spoken in the twelfth century, doesn't look at all as Anglo-Saxon did. But the spelling couldn't keep up. And from the end of the fifteenth century, English spelling began to diverge more and more from norms of English pronunciation.

Why the end of the fifteenth century? That's when the first book was printed in this country, by William Caxton. English spelling changed very little after this. When everyone started to read the same thing, a standard of spelling soon began to emerge. In fact, it took another two hundred years for the spelling system to be thoroughly established. But by the time of the first English dictionaries, in the late eighteenth century, we are dealing with a spelling system which is virtually identical with the one we use today.

Meanwhile, English pronunciation continued to change, and change ... Slowly, spelling ceased to be a reliable guide to pronunciation. And people had to learn that, if they spelled their words the way they spoke them, they would be criticized as uneducated. Incorrect spellings began to be penalized in schools. Spelling bees began to buzz. The worship of the written language had begun.

It wasn't long before people began to say: Our written language is a wonderful thing. Look how universal it is! Look how it contains our history, our laws, our literature! Look at the trouble we take to master it! Surely we ought to use it as a guide as to how we should speak?

> You should pronounce the T in *often* because there is a T in the spelling.

The wheel has turned full circle. In the beginning, we wrote as we spoke. Now, some people say, we should speak as we write.

What was happening to R, all this time?

Throughout Anglo-Saxon times, the Middle English period, and into the eighteenth century, the sound R was used both at the beginning of a word, before a vowel, as in red, ribbon, ridiculous, rum

and at the end of a word, after a vowel, as in

four, car, purr, deliver.

Shakespeare pronounced his Rs at the end of words – though you rarely hear a play performed with actors using the original pronunciation. But by the end of the eighteenth century, R ceased to be used at the ends of words in educated speech in England. No one knows why. One of those inexplicable changes in social taste. Within two hundred years, the vibrant R sound which Shakespeare used had weakened to a vowel sound, and finally disappeared altogether. The spelling, though, stayed the same. Once upon a time, if a pronunciation had gone out of use, the spelling would have gone out of use also. But not in the eighteenth century. It was too late. The spelling was fixed.

Now all of this happened only in educated speech. Since the fourteenth century, the pronunciation associated with the south-east of England, and especially that heard in the area around London, had acquired a special social status. This was where the Court was located. Anybody who was anybody in politics, the law, the church or commerce would have had an eye – and an ear – on London. People from further afield began to copy the accent, and used it in their own homes and towns. Other people began to copy them. Slowly, a prestige form of speech spread around the country – a form of speech associated with the 'best' people from the 'best' backgrounds. The pronunciation came to be used in the public schools which developed in the nineteenth century. It became an 'educated' pronunciation. Because it was widely used and understood, the BBC adopted it, in its early years, and it quickly became the voice of Britain, at home and abroad. The technical name for this voice is 'Received Pronunciation' – or R.P.

The remarkable thing about the history of R, during this period, is that most regional accents of English *kept* the R at the end of words. Think of Scottish accents, Welsh accents, Irish accents, the speech of the West country. Think of the pronunciation of most Americans. In these cases, the spelling is quite a good guide to the pronunciation. If there's an R in the spelling, it'll be sounded.

But not in R.P. Except in one circumstance. And this is where the trouble begins.

If you're an R.P. speaker, say the word *four* out loud. No R. If you're not an R.P. speaker, try to find one, and get him/her to say it out loud. No R. If you can't find one, listen to Radio 4, between half-past-three and four o'clock. The announcer will say such things as 'It's five to four'. No R.

But what if the exercise were to say *four o'clock?* If you say it yourself, you'll notice that the tip of your tongue curls back at the end of *four*, and flicks forward as you say the *o'*. There *is* an R.

Try these phrases, saying them in a natural rhythm, without a pause:

four animals	four elephants
dear Anne	dear Olive
summer evening	summer afternoon

The R at the end of each word is sounded, in R.P. It's because the next word begins with a vowel, in each case. This happens only with vowels. The R isn't sounded if the next word begins with a consonant. Try these:

four cats	four dogs
dear George	dear Jemima
summer days	summer nights

So, the rule seems clear enough. If you were teaching a foreigner to pronounce this accent of English, you could say to him:

> If there's an R in the spelling at the end of a word, pronounce it if the next word begins with a vowel, otherwise don't.

He might like to know that, when R is sounded in this way, it's called a 'linking R', in textbooks on pronunciation.

Now the interesting thing is that all these words that end in R can be grouped into six types, depending on how they rhyme. First of all, there are those words which rhyme with *more*:

> door, core, store, four, pour, implore . . .

There are so many different spellings that it's convenient to invent a new symbol, a *phonetic* symbol, to talk about the sound which all these words have in common. The symbol is /ɔː/, and it's put in special brackets, to show that we're talking about an English sound, and not a letter. The two dots show that the vowel is a long one. So, *door* would be written /dɔː/, *pour* would be /pɔː/, and so on.

Secondly, look at these words, all rhyming with *car*:

> bar, afar, star, jar, tar . . .

The phonetic symbol for this type of vowel sound is /ɑː/, as in *bar* /bɑː/, etc.

The third set of words all rhyme with *stir*:

> fir, cur, purr, infer, her ...

The phonetic symbol for this type of vowel sound is /ɜ:/, as in *fir* /fɜ:/, etc.

The fourth set of words rhyme with *fear*, where two vowels run together:

> here, leer, seer, queer, hear ...

The phonetic symbol for this type of 'double' vowel sound, or *diphthong*, is /iə/, as in *here* /hiə/, etc.

The fifth set of words rhyme with *hair*, and again two vowels run together:

> fare, fair, bear, where, care ...

The phonetic symbol for this diphthong is /ɛə/, as in *fare* /fɛə/, etc.

And lastly, there is a set of words where the end of the word is a weak 'uh' sound, usually spelled -*er*:

> bitter, butter, summer, ginger, cobbler ...

The phonetic symbol for this type of vowel sound is /ə/, as in *bitter* /bitə/, etc.

That's the lot. When there's an R in the spelling, the vowel will be one or other of these six types.

But what if there isn't an R in the spelling?

This is where 'intrusive' R comes in. R.P. speakers have got so used to sounding the R before a vowel, when the R is in the spelling, that they have unconsciously started to put one in, when there's nothing in the spelling at all. Here's a typical set of examples, all heard recently on radio or TV:

law-r and order	India-r and Pakistan
area-r of London	saw-r a crowd
armada-r of ships	trivia-r of life
America-r and elsewhere	withdraw-r-al of troops

Notice that the vowels ending the first words are the same six types as were used in the cases of 'linking' R. Don't be fooled by the way some of these words are spelled. *America* ends in the letter A, but we don't pronounce it like the A in *cat*: it's pronounced with the sound /ə/, like the *er* of *butter*.

The point to stress is that this insertion of an extra R is a perfectly natural process. You can see this from the way young children, before they get to school (and thus, learn to spell), slip these Rs quite readily into their speech. Adults who haven't learned to read do the same. They all seem to feel the need to bridge the gap after these six vowels in some way. It's as if they've 'tuned in' to the use of an R after these vowels, and always expect one to be there.

But those of us who have learned to read are in the same boat. The habit of intruding an R was laid down in childhood. We won't be able to drop it, unless we make a positive effort – and most people don't feel the need to. Even those who do wish to preserve a pure relationship between pronunciation and spelling, and who try to root out all traces of intrusive R from their speech, run the risk of failure. You can't be on guard over your speech all the time. You might be able to keep yourself from saying the more obvious cases, such as in *law and order*, or *drawing*, where the open 'aw' /ɔː/ vowel makes the presence of an R sound more noticeable. But I've never heard anyone who managed to keep R out of *all* the places where it might intrude. Especially in rapid speech, intrusive R slides in, unnoticed, unsung. I remember having a conversation with a purist student once, which went something like this:

Student: But you shouldn't say 'Africa-r and Asia'.
Self: Why not?
Student: There's no R in the spelling. It should be 'Africa and Asia'.
   I'd never put an R in.
Self: Not even in a complete sentence?
Student: Of course not.
Self: Try this one, then: 'Many countries in Africa, Asia and the
   Far East are agreed on policy.'

The student then repeated the sentence. He performed beautifully on 'Africa, Asia', putting in a slight pause and very definitely no R. But with all his attention taken up on that phrase, he forgot about the next one, and produced an equally beautiful 'Asia-r and the Far East'!

Is that the end of the story? Not quite. There's a sequel, which might be called: 'The case of the missing R'. Here's a correspondent who has been

struck by the enormous number of protests about the intrusive R, which I always notice so much. But I've missed any protests on

behalf of the 'missing' R, which I also notice in English speech –
for example, *floor, and ceiling* pronounced the same as *flaw in the
ceiling.*

So here we have the reverse process – speakers *leaving out* the R even
where there *is* an R in the spelling. Why on earth should they do that?

Left to themselves, R.P. speakers wouldn't have started to do it. But
the trouble is, they haven't been left to themselves. For over a hundred
years, the use of intrusive R has been attacked, often ferociously, by
teachers, elocutionists, and those trying to maintain a neat, regular
relationship between speech and writing. It's therefore not surprising
that many speakers – especially those who couldn't understand the basis
of the criticism in the first place – have become extremely self-conscious
about their use of R. They know that putting R in, in certain places,
can get them into trouble. They're not sure where, exactly; so, to be
on the safe side, they fall over backwards to leave R out, whenever it
occurs before a vowel at the end of a word. That way, at least (they
may subconsciously reason), they will never be blamed for an intrusive
R. But unfortunately, they go too far, and begin to leave out R even
in cases where it exists in the spelling. The result: they end up being
just as strongly criticized as if they hadn't tried to avoid the intrusive
R in the first place. There's no justice!

This kind of pendulum swing is in fact very common in the history
of language. One generation uses a sound in a certain way. The next
generation over-uses it. A third generation under-uses it. The pronunciation of R is caught up in this pendulum at the moment, and it's not
at all obvious what will happen to it next. A lot will depend on the
extent to which purist criticisms will continue to be influential, now
that society has become more tolerant of pronunciation variation in public
life. These days, all kinds of regional accents may be heard on the radio,
in parliament, and elsewhere. The kind of R.P. heard on the BBC in
its early days now sounds exaggerated and affected, to most ears. Some
radio listeners continue to be antagonized by announcers who use
intrusive R, and they let the BBC know it! So I suppose, if I were a
radio announcer, I would try to avoid cultivating a style in which intrusive
R was a noticeable feature. I'd keep clear of *draw-r-ing* and *law-r and
order*, and other words with an 'aw' /ɔː/, because they're relatively
easy to spot. I wouldn't worry quite so much about words ending in
/ə/ (see p. 41), as they tend to be less noticed. I would hope, this way,
to avoid alienating that section of my listening audience for whom such

43

things are a source of concern. After all, no one writes and complains if an announcer *doesn't* use intrusive Rs!

But if you're not a radio announcer, or some other kind of professional language user? If you're just a talker, or a listener, and your pay isn't dependent on your preserving some kind of careful linguistic identity, then should you be concerned? If the linguistic police insisted on pressing charges against R for breaking and entering, where would you stand? Guilty, or not guilty?

*

You might like to check from your own listening whether the vowel patterns described earlier are indeed the only ones that lead to an intrusive R, and make your own list of examples.

S.O.S. 2. When two wrongs make a – wrong

Many people think that language ought to be governed by rules that are as regular and unbending as are the rules of logic, or mathematics. But languages, with several hundred years of usage behind them, are never so neatly organized. There are always irregular forms, special senses, curious constructions – features which no logician would ever have invented, but which we cannot avoid whenever we speak or write.

Here's a sentence which is often judged, and condemned, by the rules of logic:

> He never said nothing.

Sentences like this one are said to have a 'double negative' construction, because they have two words going together which both express the meaning 'no' – in this case, *never* and *nothing*. But, the argument goes, if this sentence was intended to mean 'He didn't say anything', then you shouldn't use this sort of sentence. Two negatives make a positive. If he *never* said *nothing*, this must mean he *did* say *something*. Such sentences are therefore illogical and ought to be exterminated.

This judgement is indeed a harsh one. Let's look at the facts of usage, and see if there's a less extreme line to take.

First fact: this kind of double negative construction isn't used in adult standard English – unless, of course, the speaker is deliberately 'taking off' a regional dialect, to be funny. It is, however, universally used amongst the young children of standard English speakers. All children pass through a stage when they spontaneously try out such constructions. Here are some, taken from a recent recording of a three-year-old:

> Him not got no apples.   You don't want it no more.

and the beautiful

> You bettern't not do that or mummy won't give you none.

This usage is still around by the time a child gets to school, and it will turn up in his classroom speech and in his early writing. Schoolteachers

45

who are concerned to establish standard English usage in their children will have this construction in their sights from an early stage. Standard English-speaking parents don't like it either. They readily correct it when they hear it in their children. I heard one parent tell off her child for using it. She called the construction 'common'.

She was right, in a sense. So, fact number two: this kind of double negative construction is universally used outside standard English. All the regional dialects I've ever heard make use of it. It's one of the features of language which cuts across dialect boundaries. You'll be just as likely to hear it in Liverpool or London, New York or Brisbane. If it's illogical to use it, an awful lot of people are being illogical all the time. The majority of English speakers, in fact.

And fact number three: many languages do have a double negative construction as standard use. Classical Greek did. French uses a construction with more than one negative word. And even English itself used to use it routinely. Chaucer's knight, for instance, is described thus (using modern spelling):

He *never* yet *no* villany *ne* said
In all his life, unto *no* manner wight (= person).

And Hamlet says to the players:

Nor do *not* saw the air too much with your hand, thus . . .

These cases suggest that there might be a different kind of rule that languages sometimes follow – a rule like

If you want to emphasize a negative meaning, then the more negative words you put in, the better!

That view has a logic in it, too.

So, if you don't like double negative constructions, because you're a standard English user, then that's your privilege. You've been brought up that way. But don't fall into the trap of thinking that there's something intrinsically more logical about speaking or writing in that way. Or go searching for ambiguities where there are none to be found. If someone says *I ain't got no money*, he'll never be misunderstood. Would you really wish to argue that this speaker is saying that he *has* got *some*?

If someone wants to speak or write standard English, then, he's got to learn to avoid this kind of double negative construction, otherwise he'll be severely criticized. But the critics must learn to criticize for the right reasons: it's socially unacceptable, but it isn't illogical.

Two points remain. Don't forget that you do have to watch your negatives in standard English when the construction of your sentence becomes complicated, otherwise you'll get into a real tangle of meaning. Take this sentence, used in a recent speech:

> You should not think that there are no cases where a strike might not be warranted.

What on earth is going on? Is the speaker using his negatives logically, as in an algebra exercise, and wanting each one to cancel out? Or is he simply stockpiling negatives for a dramatic effect? The listener has no time to make his mind up. This kind of thing can be very confusing, and it is usually rightly criticized by manuals of usage. Don't use negatives where a positive would do, they say.

And lastly, don't forget the way some types of double negative can add a nuance of meaning. 'I shouldn't bother going to the meeting,' said a wife to her husband, to which he replied, 'I can't not go – I've got to organize the raffle.' Here, 'can't not' doesn't equal 'can'; it means something like 'must'.

*

Here are some more examples of this kind of thing, for you to react to. Each question below has a range of answers. Use the scale to mark where you think the meaning of each answer lies. Is it definitely a 'yes' answer? definitely a 'no' answer? or somewhere in between? There's a space below to add any other double negative usages you've spotted yourself.

		Definite YES	*Definite* NO
Will he arrive by tomorrow?	It's possible.		....
	It's impossible.		....
	It's not possible.		....
	It's not impossible.		....
What's she like?	She's attractive.		....
	She's unattractive.		....
	She's not attractive.		....
	She's not unattractive.		....

		Definite YES	*Definite* NO
Is it a reliable car?	It's reliable.	....	
	It's unreliable.	....	
	It's not reliable.	....	
	It's not unreliable.	....	
Does he preach interesting sermons?	They are interesting.	....	
	They are uninteresting.	....	
	They aren't interesting.	....	
	They aren't uninteresting.	....	

What should I say when I want to go to the – well, er, you know?

Call a spade a spade? By all means, if there's an obvious name for the object in question. But what if an object has several possible names? Or several dozen possible names? Then what do you call it?

And what do you say when you're not sure if you should be talking about it anyway?

Such questions are often raised in relation to the three high-risk topics in language use – excretion, death and sex. I'll leave sex till later, and start with the first.

Many languages have developed complex forms of expression in order to talk about – or rather, *not* talk about – the daily routine of coping with the human body's natural functions. English has over a hundred (I stopped counting at a hundred) words, phrases and roundabout ways of talking about this topic. And with so many to choose from, it's not surprising that people sometimes get concerned and confused. One person wrote:

> What should I say when I'm at someone else's house, and I want to go to the loo? I'm scared stiff of saying something which might offend ...

Another writer asked:

> I'm never sure, when I have people in for a meal, how to ask them whether they want to visit the bathroom, or whether I should raise the matter at all ...

Whether to raise the matter at all ...? That kind of decision isn't just a question of language. There are problems of tact and etiquette too. Problems of timing, for example. Presumably the following conversation would not usually be considered socially appropriate:

> (*Doorbell rings*)
> Host: Hello, John. Nice to see you!

49

Guest: Hi! Sorry we're a little late.
Host: That's all right. Would you like to visit the bathroom?

A little soon?

Nor, it seems, is it appropriate to interrogate a group systematically on the point, even when the timing might be right:

Hostess: Dinner'll be ready in a moment.
Host: Would you like to visit the bathroom, Jemima?
Jemima: No, thank you.
Host: Would you, Arthur?
Arthur: No, thanks. I'm fine.
Host: Mabel?
Mabel (*who has been talking to Fred*): Beg pardon?
Host (*loudly*): I was wondering whether you wanted to visit the bathroom.

The only occasion I can think of where this kind of dialogue would be at all plausible is in the middle of a children's tea-party, after lots of fizzy pop.

For adult occasions, the most acceptable remarks seem to be statements, rather than questions, with the use of an indefinite pronoun, such as *anyone*, and the speaker addressing the whole room. For instance:

Host: Bathroom first on the right, if anyone needs it.

Very important here, of course, to look around the whole group, or to look at no one at all, while saying this. Try saying it while staring at one person only! I did, on various occasions, to see what would happen, and got the following answers:

Guest 1 (*a friend*): Why pick on me? There's nothing wrong with me, you know! (*Laughs all round*)
Guest 2 (*a friend*): I don't know. I'll ask them! (*Laughs all round*)
Guest 3 (*new acquaintance*): Er, No, thank you. (*Said with some embarrassment*)

The speakers in these extracts may have dropped the linguistic equivalent of a brick, but at least they knew what they were talking about, and their listeners did too. They all opted for the idiom *to use/visit the bathroom*, which is among the most popular expressions in current use. This avoids the real issue nicely, by allowing those who find the topic embarrassing to shelter behind one prong of the ambiguity. But do remember, if you use this idiom, that it can sometimes let you down. For instance, it won't be a particularly useful idiom if you find yourself in a part of the English-speaking world where the room containing the lavatory is *never* the same as the one containing the bath – or where there aren't any baths. And you have to watch out for occasions like this:

> British visitor: May I visit your bathroom?
> Texas housewife: But certainly! I'll come with you.

(It emerged that the lady had just installed a new step-in bath in its own room, and was extremely proud of the innovation.)

In Britain, and thus in British English, a 'bathroom' usually contains a bath – but it may not contain a lavatory. In America, the room does not have to have a bath at all – and it almost always contains a lavatory. This leads to differences in usage – in restaurants, for example. You might well hear the following, in an American restaurant:

> Can you direct me to the bathroom?

You'd never hear this in a British restaurant – unless, I suppose, the diner had just had the soup poured over him!

The same sort of problem can arise over *to wash your hands*. The following conversation actually happened:

> Guest (*arriving at house late*): I'd like to wash my hands.
> Host (*knowingly*): The toilet's at the end of the hall.
> Guest: But I really do want to wash my hands. I just had to change a tyre.

So did this one:

> Hostess: Would you like to wash your hands?
> Foreign guest, with limited English (*looks at hands, carefully turning them over, to check*): No, thank you. But I should like to pee.

All right, he was foreign, and he didn't realize that *pee* is not used in formal or polite situations. But I'm sure that *to wash your hands* is just as alien an idiom to many mother-tongue speakers of English. Do *you* use it? Or do you find the phrase uncomfortable in some way?

If you don't like any of the above, then what *do* you say? Here's an exercise. Imagine yourself at a friend's new house, and you wish to – you know. You don't know where the relevant place is, so you have to ask. There's just you and the friend in the room. What do you think you would say, to complete such a sentence as the following:

Where's the — ?

Write it in, perhaps, before you change your mind.

But now, reflect. When you chose your word, did sex affect your choice? By which I mean, What word do you think you would use, if:

    (i) you are male, talking to a male friend?
    (ii) you are male, talking to a female friend?
    (iii) you are female, talking to a female friend?
    (iv) you are female, talking to a male friend?

One male person I asked claimed to use *toilet* for both (i) and (ii). Another said *bog* for (i) and *toilet* for (ii). One lady informant said *loo* for both (iii) and (iv). Another said *loo* for (iii) and *W.C.* for (iv).

Or, ask husband and wife pairs to answer two of these questions for themselves, and then to write down what they think their partners would say. In my experience, the answers often don't coincide.

When you start investigating usage in this way, you quickly uncover a complicated social and linguistic world. *Lavatory* was widespread, several years ago, and for many the only socially acceptable form. It is still used, especially by older people, and in formal speech and writing; but *toilet* is nowadays the most common 'neutral' form, along with all the phrases in which it plays a part – *toilet roll*, *toilet paper*, and so on. *Loo* has spread like wildfire in Britain, in recent years, but it remains informal.

It's worth noting that these words can be used both for the relevant item of furniture, and for a room containing this as its main or only furnishing – a potential ambiguity which doesn't usually seem to give rise to problems of communication. Compare:

I've finished painting the bathroom. Next week I'm going to do the toilet/loo.

(It could only be the room, one supposes.)

We need a plumber to fix the upstairs toilet/loo. It's leaking again.

(It could only be the item of furniture.)

On the other hand, look what happened in this conversation:

Wife (*unloading a box of shopping, containing several bottles of disinfectant*): Would you put some disinfectant in the loo?

*Husband goes upstairs, pours some down, and returns to kitchen, with
   the bottle.*

Wife: No, I said we need that in the loo, dear.

Husband: I just did!

*

What would you say in other situations, when the Question arises? Try
the following exercise. On the left-hand side, there's a brief outline of
a social setting. On the right is a list of possible expressions. The idea
is to choose one (or more) of the expressions that you think would match
the setting, if you were asking the question 'Where's the —?'. A tip:
it's often easier to decide what you definitely *wouldn't* say, rather than
what you might say.

	Definitely would say	Might say	Definitely would not say	
1. You are at a dance, in the best hotel in your town. You approach one of the staff, and ask.				A. Lav B. Toilet(s). C. W.C. D. Gents'/ Ladies'. E. Bathroom. F. Public conveniences.
2. Your are in a pub. After several drinks, you approach the lady behind the bar, and ask.				G. Loo. H. Lavatory. I. Gents'/ Ladies' toilet.
3. You are in the High Street. You approach a traffic warden, and ask.				J. Conveniences. K. Gentlemen's/ Ladies' cloakroom. L. Other.

53

You'll perhaps have noticed that, in suggesting these exercises, I've phrased my questions and comments rather carefully:

> What word *do you think* you would say ...?
> One person *claimed* to use ...

It's worth remembering a Very Important Principle, when thinking about your own use of English:

> WHAT YOU THINK YOU SAY, AND WHAT YOU ACTU-
> ALLY SAY, ARE OFTEN TWO VERY DIFFERENT THINGS.

Or, putting this another way: it's wise to avoid using either of the following, in discussing problems of English usage:

> I *always* say ...
> I *never* say ...

You may be right, but it's as well to check first.

But how to check? Simply by listening to what goes on in everyday conversation – to yourself, as well as to others. You might even start jotting down some of the variations which have turned up, if you can recall them later. A few days' listening, recently, produced the following list, in addition to the words and phrases already mentioned. It's by no means complete, so I've left space for you to add other items you may come across. In each case, I've given a brief note of the context in which the expression was used – and there's a little more space, in case you encounter the item in a different kind of context, and want to jot it down.

Other contexts?

john (American informal, heard in a TV film)

powder room (British hotel lobby, used by older lady)

craphouse (group of British teen-agers, in a pub)

rest room (American formal, in a restaurant)

men's room (British hotel lobby, used by young man)

lavvy (Scots child)

it (British housewife, to guest
who has said *Excuse me*,
while leaving the room: *It's
down the hall*)

no language, just a hand in the
air (school classroom, infants)

I *didn't* hear the following, but *you* might: *latrines, jakes, comfort station, privy, urinal, necessary house, smallest room in the house*. Nor was I counting other kinds of roundabout expression, such as *spend a penny, take a leak, need a bottle* (said in a hospital bed), or the whole range of children's slang, vulgar slang, jocular remarks and pet family names. There's no dictionary which lists them all. You have to start compiling your own.

'Good afternoon, I **had** come on behalf of the Dyslexia Society.'

Which is it? Round 2

11. He was very $\begin{Bmatrix} \text{complementary} \\ \text{complimentary} \end{Bmatrix}$ about my appearance. _____

12. I think what he's done is really $\begin{Bmatrix} \text{contemptible} \\ \text{contemptuous} \end{Bmatrix}$ _____

13. I've just complained to the $\begin{Bmatrix} \text{council} \\ \text{counsel} \end{Bmatrix}$ again. _____

14. I think that's a very $\begin{Bmatrix} \text{credible} \\ \text{credulous} \end{Bmatrix}$ story. _____

15. The shop will $\begin{Bmatrix} \text{definitely} \\ \text{definitively} \end{Bmatrix}$ deliver tomorrow. _____

16. I really $\begin{Bmatrix} \text{deprecate} \\ \text{depreciate} \end{Bmatrix}$ the use of the police on such occasions. _____

17. There's a $\begin{Bmatrix} \text{distinct} \\ \text{distinctive} \end{Bmatrix}$ possibility that he'll leave. _____

18. What about the country's $\begin{Bmatrix} \text{economic} \\ \text{economical} \end{Bmatrix}$ growth? _____

19. Is there an $\begin{Bmatrix} \text{electric} \\ \text{electrical} \end{Bmatrix}$ fault? _____

20. He's a very $\begin{Bmatrix} \text{eminent} \\ \text{imminent} \end{Bmatrix}$ man. _____

(Solutions are on p. 121)

Is this something up with which we must put?

This is a question about prepositions, not the state of the nation. But perhaps I ought not to start so abruptly, for in my experience the term 'preposition' tends to put people off. It's not as obvious a notion as 'noun' or 'verb'. One lady correspondent wrote:

> I have never been able to assimilate so much as the rudiments of grammar. Countless times my daughter has explained the difference between a noun and a pronoun, a verb and an adverb. I always say 'Thank you darling, I think I have it now'. But within minutes I've forgotten again. To me, a preposition was always the placing of one's left foot in a stirrup, before throwing one's right leg over the back of a horse.

The writer may not have known how to define a preposition, but she evidently had great skill in using them. Take her last sentence. It has half a dozen excellent prepositions:

to me	*of* one's left foot	*in* a stirrup
before throwing	*over* the back	*of* a horse

So what job do these prepositions do?

> Foot *in* the stirrup? Leg *over* the back? Back *of* a horse?

The main job of a preposition is to relate one word or phrase to another, so as to express a particular kind of meaning. Which meaning? The most common meanings expressed by prepositions are to do with space and time. *In* and *over* illustrate space prepositions. *Before* illustrates a time one. And other meanings can be expressed too – the *of* examples express 'possession', for instance.

One way of compiling a list of prepositions is to take a sentence containing one of the above prepositions, and find all the words that could replace it. They'll be prepositions too. Take the sentence:

> There was an awful noise on the bus.

What can go instead of *on? Under, near, behind, in, by, in front of ...*

Most prepositions are single words. A few consist of two or three words, such as *in front of*. Some others like this are:

> along with, out of, because of, by means of, in charge of, in accordance with.

A very useful part of speech, in short. How could it possibly upset people?

By not knowing its place.

For nearly three hundred years, popular English grammars and textbooks on style have devoted space to the question of where prepositions should go in sentences. Not in cases like *in a stirrup*, of course, where there's no choice in the matter. You can't say *a stirrup in*. The problem is raised only when prepositions turn up at the ends of sentences, as in:

> There's the town John went to.
> Have you found the bag you were looking for?

Ending sentences with prepositions, wrote one correspondent, is 'ugly'. Others have called it 'awkward'. John Dryden, the seventeenth-century poet, who also wrote a grammar of English, called it 'not elegant'.

Now I mention John Dryden, because he seems to have been the first writer to have been upset by prepositions in this way. Indeed, when he came to see it as a fault in the language, he went so far as to revise much of what he had written previously, and changed the prepositions around. For instance, instead of

> the age I live in

he wrote

> the age in which I live.

It wasn't long before the issue caught the attention of other grammarians. In particular, it impressed Lindley Murray, who was the author of a grammar book used in British schools in the late eighteenth century. He put a recommendation about the matter into his rules of grammar, and other writers followed his lead. Generation after generation of schoolchildren were taught the rule, and it became part of the linguistic state of mind of most educated adults.

These days, things are different. Schoolchildren may never even have been told what a preposition is – let alone where to put one. So they're usually not aware of these problems. In a way, they're lucky. They have one less thing to worry about, in a world where there are far more important things to be getting on with. They're no worse off than the pre-Dryden children of the early seventeenth century, who didn't know about misplaced prepositions either.

The puzzle is: Why did Dryden think it necessary to *invent* the rule in the first place?

If you look at the way Dryden himself would have learned about English grammar, one thing is very clear. The approach was entirely based on Latin. In those days, everyone who was educated knew Latin, and they used the terms and techniques of Latin grammar in order to talk about English, as in the case of split infinitives (p. 28). Many people went so far as to judge English by the standards of Latin, which they saw as a model of linguistic excellence and elegance.

Now, in Latin, you hardly ever get a preposition coming at the end of the sentence. Dryden and the others therefore assumed that, as Latin didn't do it, English shouldn't either. Any sentence which didn't live up to Latin standards in this way, it was claimed, suffered in elegance and strength of style. So don't end sentences with prepositions! Cholmondley Minor, you will write out a hundred times . . .

But is it true that a sentence ending with a preposition is felt to be clumsy or weak in its style? It may have been true for Latin, but is it true for English, which is a language constructed along very different lines?

Not usually. Throw out a net, and pull in a sample of English usage, and you'll readily find sentences where the end is the only natural or idiomatic place for a preposition to go. You might catch this one, for instance:

What are you going to cut down on?

Would anyone other than an arch-pedant say:

Down on what are you going to cut?

This is where Winston Churchill comes in – and the title of this chapter. Apparently he once made a marginal note, with reference to a sentence which avoided the prepositional ending in a clumsy way;

This is the sort of English up with which I will not put.

At the other extreme, there have been competitions to see who could produce the sentence with most prepositions at the end. One of the best turns up in a footnote in Sir Ernest Gowers' manual of style, *Plain Words*:

> What did you bring that book I don't like to be read aloud to out of from up for?

And several authors quote the two verses which the American poet Morris Bishop wrote for the *New Yorker* in 1947:

> I lately lost a preposition;
> It hid, I thought, beneath my chair
> And angrily I cried, 'Perdition!
> Up from out of in under there'.

> Correctness is my vade mecum,
> And straggling phrases I abhor,
> And yet I wondered, 'What should he come
> Up from out of in under for?'

Nor is this a modern trend. People were ending sentences with prepositions B.D. (Before Dryden), and they have continued to do so A.D. You'll find them so used in all the best authors, and all the second-best. You'll recall this one, for instance, taken from what is perhaps the most famous speech in the English language:

> Who would fardels bear,
> To grunt and sweat under a weary life,
> But that the dread of something after death,
> The undiscovered country from whose bourn
> No traveller returns, puzzles the will,
> And makes us rather bear those ills we have
> Then fly to others that we know not of?

This is *Hamlet*, Act III, Scene 1.

Given this kind of precedent, what should an aspiring grammarian do? Recommend the opposite? *Always* end sentences with prepositions? That would be going far too far.

Sometimes, Dryden's view is right – but only sometimes. Take this sentence:

> That's the place which I'd like to spend as much of my retirement as possible in.

61

I doubt whether anyone would find this an easy sentence to say. Its rhythm bounces along quite nicely – until you get to *possible*, and then you're let down with a bump. A more acceptable alternative would be to say:

> That is the place in which I would like to spend as much of my retirement as possible.

But this is rather formal. What if you didn't want to sound formal? Then you'd have to rephrase – using *where*, for instance:

> That's the place where I'd like to spend as much of my retirement as possible.

Notice, in passing, that the awkward effect of having the preposition at the end is diminished if you shorten the sentence. It's less clumsy to say:

> That's the place which I'd like to spend my retirement in.

And if the sentence is shortened still further, the feeling of awkwardness all but disappears:

> That's the place to spend retirement in!

I hope it's obvious, from these examples, that the question of where to put the preposition in English can't always be answered in a simple, yes/no way. Our usage is influenced by subtle factors which are part of the situations in which we speak. The formality of the situation, in particular. For instance, if I say:

> That's the hotel I stayed in,

I'm likely to be chatting informally. But if I say:

> That is the hotel in which I stayed,

I'm more likely to be talking in a formal setting. The speech gives the impression of being more careful, more thought out, more packaged. It's speech with a tie on. Or even a uniform on. As here:

> The prisoner left his chair, on which he had been sitting, and proceeded towards the curtains, behind which he had seen the body ...

This kind of construction is less noticeable in public writing, of course, where we expect care and organization. But in speech, if the setting isn't appropriately formal, it can sound stilted and pedantic.

The opposite also holds. If you always put a preposition at the end of a sentence, this will not be noticed in colloquial speech. But it can easily sound too casual in formal speaking styles, and it will often be criticized as sloppy in written English.

The moral is plain. It's not a matter of Right *vs* Wrong. Both styles have their place in our lives – the informal and the formal. We wear different kinds of clothes, depending on the formality of the occasion. It's the same with our linguistic habits. Or should be. We all have a linguistic wardrobe in our heads, containing a fine selection of different sentence styles. It would be a pity if we chose to use only one item from it, for every occasion.

S.O.S. 3. Is this different — what you expected?

You might ask some acquaintances to complete that sentence, and see which word they use. You'll be given *from*, *to*, or *than*. The same would happen if the word *differently* were used, as in:

> Michael behaves differently — James.

The *safest* form to use is *from*. This is the traditional standard form, and the one that is recommended in the usage manuals. But when you listen to the speech of people around you, you'll probably hear *to* used more frequently, in British English. In fact, the construction with *to* has been in use at least since the sixteenth century, and turns up in the writing of many well-known authors. But it's not used in the United States. American English has its own problems.

The objections to *different to* started in the eighteenth century, as the school grammars came to be written. It was pointed out that the first syllable of *different* comes from a Latin prefix *dis-*, which is most appropriately translated as 'from'. Moreover, it was said, look at the way other, related words work in the language. One says *differ from*, not *differ to* – *distant from*, *distinct from*, and so on. *Different to* is the exception. It ought to conform.

It's an exception, all right. But it won't conform – presumably because there are other pressures in the language which are pulling it in a different direction. It might be the existence of other phrases which use *to*, such as *opposed to*, *subject to*, *similar to*. It might be ease of pronunciation – *different to* is much easier to say than the repeated *r*'s of *different from*. Whatever the reason, it's happened, and usage is divided.

Many writers on usage have been quite impressed by the frequency of *to*, and allow its use in formal English. But everyone hates *than*. Yet this construction too is often to be heard, especially in American English. So what is happening here?

You have to make a distinction between *than* when followed by a simple noun or pronoun, or by a short phrase containing a noun, and *than* when it is followed by more complicated constructions. The first case is widely criticized:

This bag is different than yours.

Although it's been used for several hundred years, it has been ferociously attacked, on both sides of the Atlantic. The attacks are less frequent in the United States these days, as respected people come to make more use of it. But most people still prefer to play safe, and use *from*.

Now let's look at the sentences where a more complex construction follows *different*. These are sentences such as:

That's a very different argument than was used by Jim last week.

From is recommended as the standard form, here as elsewhere, but many people find it awkward, as you have to say something like:

... from that which was used by Jim last week.

That is why, on p. 12 of this book, I wrote 'it's often a different kind of meaning than many people expect'. For me, the use of 'from that which' would have been too cumbersome, and I hoped that by using *than* I was choosing the lesser of two evils. Did I succeed? If you did not even notice, then yes. If you underlined it, physically or mentally, in red ink, then no.

*

Often, when you change the preposition after a word, you change the meaning as well. Take the example of *agree*, just mentioned. You'll get a sense of the different meanings, if you complete each of the following sentences, choosing A, B or C.

1. They agree with —   A. John.
2. They agree on —   B. a price.
3. They agree to —   C. a ceasefire.

I think (1) has to be followed by A, but there's divided usage over B and C. My preference is 2–B and 3–C, but I know many people who prefer the opposite.

Begin can be used with three prepositions also. Try this:

1. I began at —   A. a new play.
2. I began with —   B. an overture by Rossini.
3. I began on —   C. Oxford.

You'll find that the meanings involved are to do with 'starting out', 'taking first' and 'starting work'.

Sorting out the usage of *concern* is more complicated, as you'll see if you try to complete these sentences:

1. I'm concerned about —	A. sales figures.
2. I'm concerned with —	B. John's illness.
3. I'm concerned for —	C. John's safety.

I can use A with either (1) or (2), but the meaning differs. If I say A1, I'm worried; if I say A2, it's my job. I can use B with either (1) or (2) also, with a similar difference in meaning. And I can use all three sentences with C, though for me, C3 is a little more formal than C1.

You can summarize your usage in a box diagram, like this. A tick means that the sequence is an acceptable one, for you. A cross means that it's unacceptable. And if you're not sure, use a question-mark. Here's my result for *concern*:

	A	B	C
1	√	√	√
2	√	√	√
3	×	×	√

What's yours?

	A	B	C
1			
2			
3			

Is there safety in numbers?

I keep getting confused about the number of nouns in English,

wrote one correspondent. I suppose I could have answered:

A quarter of a million, more or less,

but I don't think this would have been appreciated. My correspondent, it emerged from her examples, was not worried about totals, but about singulars and plurals. She went on:

I know nouns have a singular and a plural, but what I'm often not certain about is when to use the one and not the other.

And she added, a trifle wistfully, I thought:

I have the same problem with pronouns, too.

She's not alone. Many people have trouble with the number of nouns and pronouns, it seems. I'll be looking at pronouns in another chapter (see p. 105), but here are some typical questions about nouns.

Mr G: Which is it? 'The government *is* ...' or 'The government *are* ...'? I can never decide.

Ms L: Should one say 'lots of *fish*' or 'lots of *fishes*'? Does it matter?

Mr C: Is it *formulas* or *formulae* or *formuli*? Why isn't there just one plural, like with all the other nouns?

Mrs S: What's correct? *This data is? These data are? This datum is?* It's very confusing.

Mr D: *Dice* is plural, isn't it? So what should I say if I throw just one? It doesn't sound right to say *throw the die*. Is it worth worrying about? I give up!

No, Mr D. Don't give up. Never, as it were, say die!

Only a tiny proportion of all the nouns in English cause trouble like this. No one ever writes in and asks questions about a noun like *spider*.

There's no problem.

Singular: the spider   Plural: the spiders
Singular   Plural
 verb: the spider is ...   verb: the spiders are ...

Thousands and thousands of nouns are like this, in standard English – simple, straightforward, wouldn't hurt a fly.

There are only a couple of hundred nouns which don't behave as simply. They're the exceptions. But between them, they raise more blood pressure than the rest of the nouns in English put together. So what are they?

My first correspondent said:

I know nouns have a singular and a plural.

Actually, she was wrong. Most nouns do. But:

several nouns have a singular and no plural,
several more have a plural and no singular,
there are others that look singular but are really plural,
and others still that look plural but are really singular.

That just about covers all the possibilities. But it's time for some examples.

Here are some singular nouns that don't have plurals. You can't add an -s to them, when they have their normal meaning:

gold, silver, music, dirt

You can't say:

Look at all the dirts on the road.
I've been searching for golds in the hills.

On the other hand, if you use one of these words in a special meaning (*gold* short for 'gold medal', say), then you will find it in the plural. An athlete might say:

I've got two golds.

But this is a special sense.

Similarly, most names of people and places don't turn up in the plural. Try and add -s to these, for instance:

London, John, New York, Oxford Street.

It won't work – unless, again, you have a very special sense in mind. For example, you might decide to write a book called

Londons I have known!

where the word *London* doesn't mean simply 'the capital city of England', but something like 'different states of the city at different times or places'. Or you might conceivably find yourself talking to a roomful of people all called Janet or John. If only the males asked questions, you might end up saying:

The Janets were very quiet, but not the Johns.

Not a very common sort of sentence, however.

Now the reverse situation – nouns used in the plural, which you don't use in the singular. Only comedians, lunatics or children would come out with the second sentence in the following pairs:

A: Let's make *amends* for what's been done.
B: You make your amend now, and I'll make mine later.

A: They're calling the *banns* on Sunday.
B: Do they ever call a bann on Monday?

A: He lives in the *Hebrides.*
B: Which Hebride?

A: Eat your *greens,* like a good boy.
B: Can I eat this green, and leave that one?

You can try playing about with these next sentences, to get similar results:

We live on the *outskirts* of Liverpool.
The *remains* of your meal are in the oven.
He sent his *thanks* for the present.
The cat will soon get used to its *surroundings.*
Look at that lovely field of *oats!*
You must put a guard on the *premises.*

With these sentences, you can't remove the *-s* at the end of the word and keep the sense. If you try, you end up with a completely different word, such as *amend* or *remain* – or no word at all, as in *Hebride.*

There's another sort of word which acts like this. Look what happens when you have an object consisting of two equal parts, such as

pyjamas, binoculars, glasses, pliers, pants, jeans, scissors.

You can't say:

Pass me a binocular.

The best you can do is talk about a 'pair of' something.

There's an old joke about some of these nouns, which you may prefer not to read. *Trousers*, *pyjamas*, *tights*, and the like. 'Trousers', it is said, 'are singular at the top and plural at the bottom'.

I told you.

Next, what about words which look singular, but are really plural?

But hold on a minute, you might say. If they don't look singular – if they don't have an *-s* on the end – how do you know they're plural at all? The answer is to look at the way they join up with other words in the sentence that are obviously plural. Words like *these* and *those*, or *are* and *were*.

Take *police*. You can't say *polices*. But it's still a plural word, because you say:

The police are in the street,

and not

The police is in the street.

You can try the same thing with:

cattle, gentry, vermin.

People is also basically like this. You say:

The people are delighted with the new prince,

and not

The people is delighted with the new prince.

(Unless you meant the name of the newspaper – but then you'd have to spell it with a capital.) However, watch out for a complication. With this word, you can also add an *-s*, to give a quite different meaning, as in:

The new assembly will represent all the peoples of the world.

Peoples here means 'nations', or maybe 'ethnic groups'.

The same kind of complication turns up with *youth*. 'The youth of the world' are pleasant-sounding beings. 'The youths of the world' are not quite so palatable.

Now the reverse of this situation. Words which *look* plural, but are really singular. They all end in -*s*, but you know they're singular because of the way they join up with other words that are obviously singular. Words like *a* and *this*, *is* and *was*.

Look at *athletics*. You can't say *an athletic*. But it's still a singular word, because you say

Athletics is a wonderful sport.

and not

Athletics are $\left\{ \begin{array}{l} \text{a wonderful sport} \\ \text{wonderful sports} \end{array} \right.$

You can make similar pairs of sentences using these:

gymnastics, billiards, Athens, Wales, news.

My subject, *linguistics*, is like this. One asks: 'What *is* linguistics?'
So far, no problems of usage. *No one* says

Billiards are a nice game.
Wales are a pretty country.
Here are the 6 o'clock news.

But there are several other words in this group where usage depends on the meaning. Take the names of the various subjects of study which end in -*ics*, for example:

acoustics, mathematics, politics, statistics, ethics . . .

Should you say:

Politics is . . .   or   Politics are . . .?

The only sensible answer is:

It depends.

Politics takes a singular verb when you use the word as the name of the profession or social science:

Politics is a very rewarding life.

It takes a plural verb when you use the word to refer to someone's opinions or activities:

My politics are nothing to do with you!

Similarly, if you're adding up, you might say:

My maths are all wrong!

but later say:

Mathematics is a terribly complicated subject.

Names of some games are also like this:

bowls, darts, dominoes, draughts . . .

In the singular, it's the name of the game:

Dominoes is an infuriating game.

In the plural, it's the name of the implements you use:

His dominoes are next to his pint.

And certain diseases act in the same way:

mumps, measles, shingles . . .

You normally say:

Measles is a vile disease.

But in recent years, some speakers have begun to use the plural with these words. I've heard such sentences as:

Measles are horrid.

The illustrations so far have all been of nouns which usually lack either a singular or a plural. As you've seen, they sometimes cause a few problems of usage. But far more problems are caused by nouns whose handicap is that they seem to have an *excess* of plurals. There are quite a number of them.

When a noun has two plurals, there's usually a simple principle at work. One plural is the regular ending in -*s*, and this is always the normal, everyday, colloquial usage. The other plural has a foreign-looking ending, or sometimes no ending at all, and this is used when the circumstances are special – technical, professional, involving real or claimed expertise.

Let's begin with some animal names. If you heard someone say

Look at those lovely ducks!

where do you think he would be? And how are the ducks? Probably, he's on a river bank, or walking about a farmyard. The ducks are alive and well, and doubtless about to be fed. But if someone said

Look at those lovely duck!

where would he be? And how are the ducks? Undoubtedly, he's in a poultry shop, or out on the moors, with a gun in his hand. The ducks are dead, or about to be.

Duck, without the *-s* ending, is a professional usage. You'd expect hunters, butchers, farmers or other specialists to use it. The same applies to *crab(s)*, *reindeer(s)*, *elk(s)*, *antelope(s)*, and a few more – and to certain kinds of *fish(es)*.

Let's answer Ms L's question, in fact. Is it *fish* or *fishes*? Again, the answer is: It depends. *Fish* is the more widely used form. You use it when you're talking about fish viewed as a species or a collection. It's usual to say:

Will the oil harm the fishes?
The fish don't look very healthy.

Fishes is used only when you are talking about the different members of a group of fish, or of an individual species. Do you remember who swam and swam right over the dam? Three little *fishes*. And I once heard the following sequence, said in a house at feeding-time:

I'll just go and give the cat some fish. Which reminds me – one of those fishes hasn't eaten anything today.

The first use referred to cat-food. The second, to one of the pet goldfish.

Then there's a large number of technical plurals – usually foreign words, mainly used by specialists. This is where Mr C's question comes in. *Formulas* or *formulae*? If the man in the street wanted to talk about more than one formula, the natural thing would be to add an *-s*, and that's what most people do. But if you have to talk about more than one formula when you're doing your job, you'd use the other ending. Mathematicians and other scientists, speaking and writing as professional people, would use *formulae*. No one uses *formuli*. That's a mis-spelling, probably influenced by other irregular plurals, such as *cacti*, *fungi*, or *styli*.

These last examples are also technical. If you know about cactus plants, or wish to give the impression that you know, you will talk about *cacti*. A hi-fi buff wouldn't talk about *styluses* for his equipment. After all, one way you know he's a buff is by his use of the plural *styli*!

Similarly, *vertebrae* relates to such technical fields as medicine and biology. *The Bedouin* and *the Eskimo* are more likely to turn up in textbooks or documentaries. *Cherubim* and *seraphim* are quite definitely religious. You wouldn't expect a mother to gaze at a group of happily playing children, and exclaim:

Oh, the lovely cherubim!

There's no difference in the pronunciation of *bureaus* and *bureaux*, *plateaus* and *plateaux*; but if you use the *-x* form, you're more likely to be an antiques dealer or a geographer. Similarly, the fish expert talks about *aquaria*; the man in the street *aquariums*. Which you use depends on how much of an expert you wish to appear to be. And only the most amateur of D.I.Y. men would talk about *feet* and *inches* when going to buy some wood or nails. The expert says such things as

A four-foot length of . . .

or, when asked what length of nail,

Three inch.

Appendix and *index* are different. These nouns have developed two plurals, but the forms don't have the same meaning. With *appendix*, the form with *-s* is the one to use in medicine. The surgeon removes people's *appendixes*. If you talk about *appendices*, you must be referring to the bits of extra material which turn up at the end of a book or report. But even here, the regular form is often used. I've heard students say things like:

How many appendixes has that book got?

The usage would be frowned upon by librarians and other professionals, though.

And *index*? You'd use *indices* only when talking about certain kinds of mathematical or scientific symbol. Only books and other printed materials have *indexes*.

That leaves one other type of two-plural noun which causes regular questions about usage. These are nouns like:

club	family	group
crowd	government	pair
committee	clergy	orchestra

and some proper nouns like:

Kremlin, Parliament, the United Nations.

Grammar books usually talk about them as 'collective' nouns, because they all refer to groups, or 'collections', of people or things. They're different from all the other nouns in this chapter, because they are used in two different plural ways.

Government has the normal plural *governments.*

But in addition, you can say:

The government is ... alongside *The government are* ...

Which is correct?
   Both. Once again, it depends on what is meant.
   When you use the singular noun with a singular verb, the group is seen, impersonally, as a unit. The members of the group aren't singled out for our attention. But when the singular noun is used with a plural verb, then the members of the group *are* singled out. The group is seen as a set of individuals. It's getting personal.
   The best way of seeing this contrast in meaning is by thinking about the difference between such sentence pairs as the following:

   A. The government *is* behind the times. *It* ought to resign.
   B. The government *are* sticking together on this one. But I shouldn't be surprised if some of *them* resign.

This kind of difference is often made in British English. For some reason, it doesn't have any currency in American English. Americans seem only to say *government is.*
   You can see the same kind of distinction in:

   A. The orchestra *was* brilliant tonight.
   B. The orchestra *have* all gone home.

   A. The committee *is* to be disbanded.
   B. The committee *are* making up their minds.

Data is the king of irregular plurals, and deserves a section to itself. Originally, it was used only as a plural form:

Those data are very revealing,

one scientist might say to another. The singular was *datum* – a much rarer word, usually used in the special sense of 'point of reference'. Over the years, *data* has come to be used as a singular. You'll hear it in such sentences as:

The data *is* very revealing.
This data is the best I've seen.
We haven't *much* data on that point.

In this use, *data* refers to 'all the information we're talking about, viewed as a whole'. But when *data* is used as a plural, the meaning is more restricted. It then refers to 'several specific items of information'. I once heard a scientist say:

Our *data is* all potentially useful, but can I draw your attention in particular to *these data* on this page.

How to have your linguistic cake and eat it!

A few decades ago, writers criticized the singular use of *data* as a particularly bad grammatical error, and many people still feel this. The criticisms are less fierce today, as the usage is found in all kinds of speech styles, formal as well as informal, technical as well as popular. But the result of all the criticism has been to leave many writers – including scientists – uncertain about which form they should use. One research scientist said to me, sadly:

If I write *data is*, people will think I'm ignorant – that I don't know my classical languages. If I write *data are*, people will think I'm pedantic and stuffy.

I couldn't help. Contemporary usage is mixed, and attitudes are unclear. Conservative language users will prefer *data are*. Writers anxious to cultivate an informal style will prefer *data is*. 'What sort of linguistic image of yourself do you want to convey?' I asked the research scientist. He wasn't sure. 'Then you'd better avoid the issue, and use a different term', I said.

He did. In his next paper, he replaced 'Fresh data is needed' by 'further research is needed'. Exit one usage problem – for the time being.

If *data* is king of irregular plurals, *dice* is heir-apparent. *Dice* – the cube used in games of chance – in current English is one of quite a large set of nouns whose singular and plural forms are the same. They include:

sheep, salmon, Chinese, Japanese, innings, means, series, species

and there are several others. You just don't know, if someone says *the sheep*, how many are being referred to.

Dice is slightly different, in one respect: originally, it was a plural in its own right. The singular was *die*. But all of this was a long time ago. These days, *die* is used in this sense only in the idiom *The die is cast*. Only the person with a knowledge of language history knows that *dice* and *die* are related. In modern usage, *dice* is used both in the singular and in the plural. If you say

The dice is on the table,

you are talking about one cube. If you say

The dice are on the table,

you are talking about several cubes.

But anxious word-watchers have a long memory, and you will still find *The dice is . . .* singled out for criticism – especially in American English. I don't know what the critics say instead. Would they actually say such things as

I need a die to play this game?

Perhaps such critics don't play dice-games, so that they don't have a problem.

But the story of *dice* isn't over yet. I've heard children often – and adults occasionally – coin a *new* plural, when they want to make the distinction between one or more cubes. One person said:

You play that game with one dice, but you need two dices for the other one.

This is a perfectly natural development, in the history of language. The regular plural ending comes along to help out. It hasn't happened to *data* (yet), but it's already happened to *agenda*. Nowadays you'll hear:

The agendas are ready to be given out.

Dices isn't very widely used as yet, but who knows what another fifty years of usage will lead to?

*

There's much more to be said about singulars and plurals. You might like to listen out for some of the changes in usage that are going on in the language at present, apart from the ones I've already talked about. There's a space for your own usage, and for noting the usage of others.

Your preference   *Other people's usage*

Do you say A. *spoonsful*
           B. *spoonfuls?*

Do you say A. *handkerchiefs*
           B. *handkerchieves?*

What about *mother-in-law?* If
there were a roomful of them,
would they be A. *mothers-in-law*
           B. *mother-in-laws?*

If you had male servants, would
you call them A. *manservants*
           B. *menservants?*

Do you say A. *10 pence*
           B. *10 pennies*
           C. *10 p's*
           D. *10 p?*

And don't forget spelling and
punctuation. Do you write
           A. *MP's*
           B. *MPs?*

           A. *in the 1980's*
           B. *in the 1980s?*

Educated people use all of these. Some usages are on the increase. Some are on the decrease. Some are finely balanced. So whenever you make a note of a usage that strikes you, remember to add the relevant details, which will help you to make sense of your observations. Whose usage was it? Where did it happen? In what kind of situation? Give your attitude towards it, by all means, but aim to *explain* what is happening in the language, rather than to condemn it. And above all, keep a note of the date when you observed the usage. If you look at what you've written in a few years' time, you may be surprised at the way usage, and perhaps your own views, have changed.

Noun used	When?	By whom?	In what context?	Your attitude

'They call themselves communists and we call them communists. They call us capitalists, but we don't. Why?'

Which is it? Round 3

21. He's also a person of $\left\{ \begin{array}{l} \text{exceptional} \\ \text{exceptionable} \end{array} \right\}$ intellect. _____

22. You're quite safe. The material is $\left\{ \begin{array}{l} \text{inflammable} \\ \text{non-flammable} \end{array} \right\}$. _____

23. He's in trouble for $\left\{ \begin{array}{l} \text{flaunting} \\ \text{flouting} \end{array} \right\}$ the school rules. _____

24. It was just a $\left\{ \begin{array}{l} \text{fortuitous} \\ \text{fortunate} \end{array} \right\}$ remark, which he later regretted. _____

25. They're leaving now on their $\left\{ \begin{array}{l} \text{historic} \\ \text{historical} \end{array} \right\}$ journey. _____

26. The paper $\left\{ \begin{array}{l} \text{implied} \\ \text{inferred} \end{array} \right\}$ that the accident was avoidable. _____

27. The disease $\left\{ \begin{array}{l} \text{inflicted} \\ \text{afflicted} \end{array} \right\}$ him for years. _____

28. That's a very $\left\{ \begin{array}{l} \text{ingenious} \\ \text{ingenuous} \end{array} \right\}$ machine! _____

29. I've got a new television $\left\{ \begin{array}{l} \text{licence} \\ \text{license} \end{array} \right\}$. _____

30. $\left\{ \begin{array}{l} \text{Lightening} \\ \text{Lightning} \end{array} \right\}$ never strikes in the same place twice. _____

(Solutions are on p. 122)

Why is life so stressful?

Would you mind repeating that in words of one syllable?

No problem. 'Why – is – life – so – full – of – stress.'

But it would be rather difficult to keep up this pattern for long. Most words in English have more than one syllable. And this is where the idea of 'stress' comes in.

When you're talking about speech, 'stress' refers to the amount of loudness, or emphasis, with which you utter a syllable. If a syllable is strongly stressed, it sounds quite loud, compared to the other syllables around it. If it's weakly stressed, it sounds quite soft. You can hear the difference clearly, if you say the words out loud.

Here are some words with two syllables. In each case, the first is the louder.

female, **dan**ger, **win**dow, **ta**ble, **rhu**barb.

Here are some with the second syllable louder:

ma**chine**, Chi**nese**, di**vide**, ca**reer**, pre**pare**.

When the words have three syllables, the stressed syllable is usually the first or second. First one loudest?

yesterday, **pho**tograph, **el**ephant.

Second one loudest?

im**por**tant, de**vel**op, to**ma**to.

The third syllable is sometimes the loudest, in words like:

country-**house**, ginger-**beer**.

There's even more choice with four-syllable words. Listen to these:

1st syllable loudest: **me**lancholic **ca**terpillar
2nd syllable loudest: un**for**tunate rhi**no**ceros
3rd syllable loudest: unim**por**tant circu**la**tion
4th syllable loudest: misunder**stood** aquama**rine**

The words get bigger and bigger. Here's just a selection of longer words, each containing one main stress. Cover the right-hand side of the page before you read them out loud, and see if you can decide which it is. Then check the answers.

satisfactory	3rd – **fac**
administrative	2nd – **min**
electrification	5th – **ca**
enthusiastic	4th – **as**
internationalize	3rd – **na**

The stress pattern in English words is evidently quite complicated. In fact, it's an awful business trying to learn it. Ask any foreigner.

But there are certain guidelines, which any foreigner would be glad to follow. In particular, it's worth noticing that English is a language which has a bouncy sort of stress pattern. You hear it most clearly in the te-tum te-tum rhythm which is found in a great deal of English poetry. Remember Thomas Gray's *Elegy*?

> The curfew tolls the knell of parting day,
> The lowing herd winds slowly o'er the lea ...

You can tap the rhythm out with your fingers, quite easily. And of course more complicated rhythms too, as in the opening lines of Charles Wolfe's poem *The Burial of Sir John Moore*:

> Not a drum was heard, not a funeral note,
> As his corpse to the rampart we hurried ...

You can hear the drum in the rhythm of the speech.

Now, all forms of spoken English have a rhythm. It isn't usually as noticeable as in poetry, but it's there all the same. Say the following sentence out loud, or persuade someone else to say it, and listen to the tum-te-tum pattern emerging:

> I really think that Jack and Jill should stay the night in town.

Said with a bounce to it, you might even mistake it for a piece of (bad) poetry.

When words have more than one syllable, they too follow this tum-te-tum pattern, on the whole. Each word has one loudest stress, as we've seen, but the other syllables keep the bounce going, in a quieter way. Let's look at one of the longer words in more detail:

electrification

The *ca* is the loudest part, as you can tell from observing the way the word rhymes – in a limerick, say:

> A lady of sinister nation
> Decided to visit a station ...

I can't think what might come next, but the last line is:

> And discovered electrification.

But now, listen carefully to that last line. The word *electrification* has a second beat in it, on the syllable *lec*. Its rhythm is te-tum-te-te-*tum*-te. This extra 'tum' is important, to keep the rhythm flowing. Without it, there would be four weak 'te's together. English doesn't like lots of 'te's running together like that. There's usually a 'tum' brought in to split them up. But it's not as loud as the *main* 'tum' of the word.

Listen to the stress patterns on these words. The loudest stress is already indicated, in heavy type. See if you can spot the second-loudest stress. Cover the right-hand side of the page, if you don't want to see the answers.

te**le**phone	2nd-loudest syllable: phone
under**stand**	un
helicopter	cop
identifi**ca**tion	den
unre**li**able	un

It's possible to see the pattern of loudness in an English sentence by devising a special notation. Let's use ● for the two types of loud syllables, and • for the soft ones. What you get is something like this:

● • ● • ● • • ● • ● • • ● • • ●

You don't get this:

● • • • • ● ● • • • • ● • • • • ●

Such a pattern would sound horribly jerky to English ears. And in fact, non-fluent foreigners often talk this way.

Here endeth the phonetics lesson. But without some background information of this kind, it isn't possible to explain what's happening to word stress in modern English. And there *is* a lot happening, as listeners to the radio are very ready to point out. Here's a random selection from the correspondence:

> Mr P: Why the un-English stress on 'communal' these days?
> Mrs Q: I regret the use of 'ordinarily' – another Americanism!
> Mr R: I hate the mispronunciation of 'dispute' as 'dispute'.
> Mr S: Why 'kilometre'? We don't say 'centimetre'.
> Mr T: I have collected over a hundred wrongly stressed words used on the radio in the last few days: controversy, decade, integral, research ...

And he does, indeed, list 102 words, where, these days, sometimes one syllable is strongly stressed, sometimes the other.

But stress-hunting isn't a recent sport. Stress has been shifting up and down some English words for at least three hundred years. In the seventeenth century, for instance, words like *necessary* were pronounced in England with the strong stress on the *-ary* ending. This is the pronunciation that went to America, and of course it's the one still in use there today. People often complain about the way English speakers are increasingly using this stress pattern these days, in words like

momentarily, primarily, temporary.

Horrid Americanism, it's said. Take Mrs Q's remark, for example. The irony of the situation is that pronunciations of this kind were British first!

There have been many other words which have changed their stress pattern in the last hundred and fifty years or so. Once, people all said

revenue	Nowadays they say	revenue
illustrate		illustrate
character		character
prosperity		prosperity
convenient		convenient

No one remarks on these changes any more, because they're over and done with. Similarly, in a hundred years time, I doubt whether anyone will be worrying about the changes which are taking place now. Our great-grandchildren will be complaining to the BBC about a new set of words.

But meanwhile, a lot of people *are* worrying about the changes that are currently taking place. You can group these changes into two main types. First, there are words where the traditional main stress falls on

87

the second or third syllable. The modern tendency is to bring the stress forward, and put it on the first. Examples:

research, a defect, adult, contribute, a dispute.

The second group is much larger. This contains words where the traditional main stress falls on the first syllable. The modern tendency is to put the stress on a later syllable in the word. Examples:

controversy, integral, decade, ordinarily, aristocrat,
kilometre, inventory, prematurely, laboratory, subsidence.

Sometimes the change of stress alters the actual pronunciation of the word. The *i* of *subsidence* rhymes with *Sid*, when the stress is on the first syllable. It rhymes with *side*, when the stress is on the second.

What is going on? Why can't people be satisfied with the stress they've got? Is there anything that can be done about it?

To take the last question first. Not very much, because the changes result from linguistic forces which are little understood, and over which we seem to have little or no control. Most of the problems seem to be the result of our unconscious desire to maintain the basic, regular heartbeat of rhythm in our speech. It's as if we want to preserve as much as possible the te-tum-te-tum way of speaking. Words which fall neatly into this pattern, when they're used in speech, aren't affected. The pressure to change comes when we try to use words which *don't* fall neatly into this pattern. The word's personal stress-pattern pulls one way. The underlying heart-beat of the language pulls another way. The result? Divided usage for a while, until, in the end, the heart-beat wins.

It's an interesting theory, and it does seem to explain a lot of what happens. Take a word like *prematurely*, for instance. Its stress pattern, traditionally, is ● • • •. Said by itself, as a single word, there's no problem. But of course, words aren't used by themselves. They're put into sentences, and used alongside other words. Their stress patterns have to cooperate with those of other words, and everything has to work together to produce an acceptable sentence rhythm.

Poor old *prematurely*! It will try to preserve its ● • • • identity – or perhaps I should say, we English speakers will try to preserve this rhythm on its behalf. But it doesn't have much of a chance. It is fighting against a speech foundry which is mass-producing sentences with a • ● • ● rhythm. If it wants to be used, it will be difficult not to conform. Slowly, individual pronunciations of *prematurely* will succumb. Just once in a while, you'll perhaps hear 'prema*turely*' or '*prema*turely'. Then twice in a while. Then often.

Of course, most people are conservative about their language when they begin to think about it. Their speech patterns remind them of how they were brought up, of where they are from. Your pronunciation is part of your identity. It helps you to belong. So naturally, if you notice a change, you may well feel a reaction against it. You probably won't notice the change much, if at all, in everyday speech. But in public, and these days especially on the radio, sharp-eared people detect the change, and see it as a sign of carelessness, or falling standards. They write in and complain.

But it is already too late. If the new stress pattern has begun to be used in formal speaking situations, it must already be widespread in conversation. And as more and more respected speakers come to use the new pattern in public, when they are off their guard, it gradually becomes acceptable, then desirable – and in due course it becomes the standard form. It takes a while. A generation or two.

There's always a rearguard action, of course. And with a really ferocious attack on a new stress pattern, the process will be slowed down. Take the kind of battering which *controversy* has received in Britain. It has made people very self-conscious about their use of this word in formal speech. The BBC, for example, recommends the older stress pattern as the official pronunciation. I don't know what influence this is likely to have. Radio hasn't been around long enough for us to be able to judge whether its pronunciation standards, which originally came from society at large, will in turn influence society. Personally, I doubt it.

What no one can say is why only some words are affected by the heartbeat steam-roller, at any one time. Why should the man in the street allow the change in such words as *integral*, *exquisite*, *deficit*, *despicable*, and *controversy*, but keep saying hundreds of other words, of similar length, in the old way? After all, nothing has happened to *quantity*, *innocent* or *yesterday*.

There are lots of possible reasons. It could be something to do with who first used the new patterns in speech, and the influence that person – or group of people – had. '*Dispute*', for instance, has certainly been popularized in recent years by its frequency of use on the media, in the context of industrial negotiations.

Another reason is the way in which words affect each other. If there are lots of words in a language which pattern one way, and just a few which pattern differently, the exceptions will be under strong pressure to conform. This may well be why people are increasingly saying 'controversy' in Britain. The ● • • • pattern is widely used in English, in such words as *admiralty, difficulty, excellency*. What you have to notice about such words is that they all have two consonants before the y:

admira*lt*y   diffic*ul*ty   excelle*nc*y.

Controversy used to have two consonants here – in the days when the *r* consonant was pronounced after a vowel in English – and presumably that's why this word had the ● • • • pattern. But these days, the *r* has gone, in speech. *Controversy* has only one sounded consonant before the final vowel. So it isn't surprising to see it conforming to the stress pattern of the many other words which have only one consonant towards the end – words like

apolo*g*y   facili*t*y   rhinoceros.

Another word which is doing the same thing is *metallurgy*. In the United States, where the *r* has been retained, this change hasn't taken place. There is no controversy over *controversy*. Everyone pronounces it with the first syllable strongest.

So we can search for reasons, to explain why stress patterns change, and sometimes we find some. But there's always an element of doubt about the reasoning, because there are so many obscure factors involved. For instance, was it the influence of the verb *prefer*, with its stress on the second syllable, which led people to start saying 'preferable'? Likewise, was it the existence of *compare* which made them say 'comparable'? Very likely, but you can't be sure.

Why did 'dispute' become 'dispute'? Was it just the trade union usage? Unlikely. The change may well have been influenced by other forms of this word – forms like *disputation* or *disputant*, where the *u* is short and the *dis* is quite strong. Or perhaps people were unconsciously trying to maintain a difference between the noun *dispute* and the verb *dispute*. Some other pairs of words show a difference – the noun *record* and the verb *record*, for example. Listen to these sentences:

I've just bought a new **record**
I'm going to re**cord** the facts.

The stress keeps them apart. So why not for *dispute* too?

And what about Mr S's question. Why did 'kilometre' become 'kilometre'? This is a strange development, for it runs against the pattern of other *kilo-* words (*kilogramme*, etc.), which are all stressed on the first syllable. And, as he says, the other measuring words (*centimetre*) are stressed that way also. Obviously, some other factor must have intervened. Perhaps it was the *early* introduction of *kilometre* into English that did it. People knew about kilometres long before they had heard of other metric units. I can handle kilometres, but I still have great difficulty with kilograms, kilolitres, and the rest. So, when *kilometre* arrived, its pronunciation was quickly influenced by other measuring words which were developing – words ending in *-ometer*, such as:

thermometer, speedometer, barometer, gasometer

Now that the other *kilo-* words are coming to be more widely used, there's a pull in the reverse direction, and probably, in due course, it will win. When a new generation has learned their metric tables in school, the rhythmic parallels between

centimetre   millimetre   kilometre

are bound to restore the status quo.

If you do go stress-hunting, be on the lookout for variations due to regional accent differences. There are lots of differences in stress in Scots English, for instance. In Scotland, you'll be able to hear:

enquiry   instead of   en**quiry**
realize   instead of   rea**lize**
ad**vertise**   instead of   **ad**vertise.

Also, keep an ear open for words which have two stress patterns, *both* of which are standard. The difference is to do with grammar. When these words are used in one part of the sentence, they have one stress pattern. When used in a different part, they have another. For instance, say these two sentences out loud:

I think you're altogether wrong.
There were about fifty altogether.

When *altogether* is used before the word it goes with, you put the stress on the first syllable ('**al**together'). When it's used after the word it goes with, the stress is on the third syllable ('alto**ge**ther'). You can hear a similar distinction on the word *absolutely*:

I **ab**solutely agree!
I agree abso**lu**tely!

Sometimes, changing the stress produces a difference in meaning. How would you say the following sentences, for instance?

The people are already in the hall.
The people are all ready in the hall.

In written English, the two phrases are spelled differently, of course. But in speech, it's the stress pattern which does it. The first sentence has a weak stress on *al-*. The second has a strong stress on *all*. You can play about with *alright* and *all right* in a similar way. And with *everyday/every day*, *everyone/every one*, *no one* (= nobody)/*no one* (= no one person) ...

These days, you're supposed to try to cope with life's stresses, not fight against them. The principle applies to linguistic stresses, too.

*

You might like to keep a special note of words and phrases where a change of stress leads to a change of meaning. Here are a few I've made up. There's space opposite for you to add others.

I refuse to collect the refuse.

  · ●   ● ·

I expect good conduct when I conduct.

       ● ·   · ●

Soldiers shouldn't desert in the desert.

        · ●   ● ·

I can see a toy factory. Which is it?	A. A factory which *makes* toys.
● · · ·	B. A factory which *is* a toy.
I can see a toy factory. Which is it?	A. A factory which *makes* toys.
● ● · ·	B. A factory which *is* a toy.
The German teacher has arrived. Which is it?	A. A teacher *of* German.
● · · ·	B. A teacher who *is* German.
The German teacher has arrived. Which is it?	A. A teacher *of* German.
● · ● ·	B. A teacher who *is* German.

'I'm warning you for the last time Mac.

"Hopefully" is an adverb.'

S.O.S. 4. Hopefully, the last word

No, it's the first word – that's the trouble. The objections are to sentences such as:

> Hopefully, the play will start in London next Friday.
> Hopefully, sales will improve next year.

It's not possible to start hopefully, or improve hopefully, it is said. It's an improper usage. Adverbs are supposed to limit the meaning of verbs, as in *He ran quickly* – the *quickly* tells you something about the *running*. *Hopefully* is an adverb, but it tells you nothing about the meaning of the verbs *meet* or *improve*, in these sentences. So, critics conclude, it's just a sloppy way of talking, which should be replaced by more careful constructions based on the verb *hope*, as:

> Let us hope that sales will improve next year.
> It is to be hoped that they'll improve.
> I'm hopeful that they'll improve.

Why *hopefully* should have attracted all the criticism is a puzzle. After all, there are several other adverbs which are used at the beginning of a sentence in this way, and they haven't been criticized:

> Naturally, I'd like you to stay with us for a few days.
> Amazingly, he arrived on time.
> Fortunately, the bus wasn't late.
> Funnily enough, I'd been thinking about that.

They all express some kind of judgement on the part of the speaker. Sometimes they occur at the beginning of a sentence. Sometimes they occur in the middle or at the end, as in:

> He could stay over in town, *possibly*?
> They've *certainly* got no reason to complain.

They are often several words long:

> To my regret ..., Even more important than that ...,

It must be something to do with the way in which *hopefully* first came to people's attention. Something about this word must have upset them. Some people think that the antagonism stemmed from the way in which German immigrants to the U.S.A. used it in their speech, as a translation of *Hoffentlich* ... British criticism is largely on the grounds that the phrase is distinctively American, and to be avoided therefore. Kingsley Amis gave 'floating *hopefully*', as he called it, a real panning once, in an article he published in 1980 called 'Getting It Wrong'. The fellow who uses it, he says,

> can't say 'I hope' because that would imply he has surrendered control of events; he can't really use J. F. Kennedy's favorite, 'I am hopeful that', without being J. F. Kennedy; he can't say 'with luck' which is all he means; so he says 'hopefully' and basks in a fraudulent glow of confidence.

I think this is a little extreme. After all, the language may be developing a *useful* distinction here, enabling us to sharpen our thinking. For instance, recently I came across the following comment:

> Hopefully, the election result will be announced by 11 o'clock, and *I* hope it will too.

The first part of the sentence seems to express a *general* point of view – everyone was hoping that the result would be announced by 11, not just the speaker. The second part, by contrast, expresses the spokesman's personal opinion.

It's too soon to say what's going to happen to *hopefully*. It might survive, or it might die the death of a cliché. Usage warning signs are only now beginning to be put up in dictionaries. There's some life in the old word yet.

*

But remember, it's not just *hopefully* that's involved. Here are other adverbs I've heard at the beginning of a sentence. Do you find that they raise the same problems?

	Acceptable?	Unacceptable?
Thankfully, they all arrived home together.		
Happily, he found his keys.		

Regrettably, it rained.

Very wisely, he stayed at home.

Funnily enough, I saw John the next day.

Incredibly, he survived.

Luckily, she had enough money.

Others?

What has sex got to do with it?

If sex rears its head everywhere these days, as is often suggested, then it should come as no surprise to find a chapter on it in this book. But you might be surprised to see that it's the largest chapter. This is not a commercial manoeuvre. It's simply a reflection of the fact that, these days, some of the most interesting – and awkward – problems of English usage stem from modern society's changing attitudes to sex, and to the sexes. *Vive la différence?* But how, exactly, in contemporary English?

When linguists approach the topic of sex – in their books, at any rate – they do something which at first sight seems very strange. They don't usually refer to 'sex' at all. Instead, they talk about 'gender'. 'Masculine' and 'feminine' genders, for instance. Nouns, adjectives and often other parts of speech are said to be masculine, or feminine, and often 'neuter' is used as well.

There's nothing prudish about this. There's a good reason why you have to talk about 'gender' rather than 'sex' when you're looking at a language. It's because the genders that turn up in a language don't necessarily have anything to do with sex at all. Words that are 'masculine gender' often don't refer to male beings. 'Feminine gender' words are often not female.

But why talk about 'gender' at all? Where do labels like 'masculine' and 'feminine' come from?

When you're teaching or learning a language, it's very important to have some way of sorting out the different patterns of grammar or vocabulary which are used. For instance, if you were learning French, one of the first things you'd notice is the way that all the nouns in the language fall into one of two types. When you want to say '*the* something-or-other', you find that there are thousands of words which go with *le*, and thousands more which go with *la*. *Le* words include:

   le fromage   'cheese'   le sexe   'sex'.

La words include:

> la pomme   'apple'   la poche   'pocket'.

You've got to get it right, if you want your French to be acceptable. *Le pomme* sounds awful, to a Frenchman.

When grammarians first wrote their books on French grammar, they had to give names to these two types of word. They could have called them anything. Type I and Type II words, for instance. Or A words and B words. But they chose the labels 'masculine' and 'feminine', because that's the way it was done in the grammars of Latin and Greek before them. It's only because Latin grammar became so widely known that everyone thinks of gender in these terms still. We owe so much of our thinking and terminology about language to the pioneering work of the Roman and Greek thinkers, two thousand years ago.

If a language has *three* main patterns for its nouns, the same approach is used. The first two are called 'masculine' and 'feminine', and the third is called 'neuter', again following Latin. This is the case in modern German, for instance, where there are three types of nouns.

The important point to appreciate, in all of this, is that the patterns into which these words fall don't necessarily have anything to do with the sex of the beings or objects referred to. There's a certain tie-up, of course, otherwise the terms 'masculine' and 'feminine' wouldn't have been chosen in the first place. But whenever you come across a language where its words pattern in this way (not all languages have gender – Chinese or Japanese, for instance), *don't* expect everything to be logical. It would be nice if the only words to be masculine were the names of male human beings and animals. The only feminine words were the names of female humans and animals. And neuter words were everything else. But it's not like that. Languages aren't so logical.

Let's take German. Large numbers of inanimate objects are masculine or feminine. A 'timetable' is masculine (*der Fahrplan*), but a 'ticket' is feminine (*die Fahrkarte*). 'Winter' is masculine (*der Winter*), but 'autumn' is feminine (*die Herbst*). No one has ever been able to work out a 'logic' for such things. Nor is it obvious why the nouns referring to several females are neuter in gender, and not feminine at all! The word for 'girl' is neuter (*das Mädchen*). So is the word for 'young lady' (*das Fräulein*). Curious!

In English, fortunately, things are a lot simpler! There's no gender as there is in French or German. *The* stays *the*, and it can be used with almost every noun in the language. It wasn't always like this. In Anglo-Saxon times, there were genders similar to those used in German – and several forms of the word *the*, for instance. But these days, gender has all but disappeared. The only way you could group nouns into gender types today is by seeing how they pattern in relation to such pronouns as *he*, *she* and *it*. And when you sort them out like this, you find that the types are pretty logical. In English, gender and sex do go very well together. They make a lovely couple.

Let's look at the various types. First, there are the words which go with *he* – the 'masculine' words, if you want to use the old terminology. Examples? *Man*, *boy*, *king*, *monk*. We say:

Do you see that *man*. *He*'s …

Then there are words which go with *she* – 'feminine', if you like. *Woman*, *girl*, *queen*, *nun*. We say:

Do you see that *woman*. *She*'s …

The vast majority of words in English go with *it*: *box*, *table*, *chair*, *egg*, *information* … You might call them 'neuter' – but most modern grammars refer to them as 'inanimate' words (as opposed to the 'animate' male and female ones).

Not many of these words show their gender in their endings. A few of the *he*-words do:

bridegroom (as opposed to *bride*)
widower (as opposed to *widow*).

And quite a large number of *she*-words do:

hostess (as opposed to *host*)
waitress (as opposed to *waiter*)
heroine (as opposed to *hero*).

The -*ess* ending is the main one. And here we meet a usage problem, for the way in which people use words with the -*ess* ending is slowly changing, along with changing attitudes to female roles in society. Once upon a time, the -*ess* ending had no emotional overtones. A *poetess* was simply a female poet. These days, several -*ess* forms are felt to be unpleasant or condescending. I doubt whether many people today use *negress* or *jewess*, for example. These two forms are particularly disliked in the U.S.A. Many female authors don't like to be referred to by the word *authoress* – and the same applies to *poetess* and *sculptress*. I've sometimes heard actresses get very upset when labelled as *actresses*, as opposed to *actors*.

It seems to be mainly the artistic professions in which the changes are most noticeable. I've never heard waitresses, stewardesses or heiresses get upset about their labels – and duchesses, empresses, goddesses and other high-ups remain unaffected. *Heroine* causes a few problems. People quite often say things such as 'She's the real hero of that situation'. *Heroine*, to many, is beginning to sound like something out of a Victorian girls' adventure comic.

But -*ess* is alive and well, as an ending. You can always tell when a bit of language is healthy, because it gets used in new and creative ways. So it's a sign of good constitution to hear a TV comic make a joke recently, in which he talked about a vicar's wife as a 'vicaress'.

Another way of indicating gender in a word is to add another word to it that is clearly 'he' or 'she'. For instance, there's no way of telling whether any of the following nouns are male or female:

cousin, fool, friend, guest, neighbour, student.

There's a 50–50 chance of fools, friends, guests and the others being male – or female. The ambiguity can sometimes cause surprises.

You didn't tell me your cousin was a girl!

is a line from (at least) one love story.

If you want to specify sex with words like this, you have to add another word – something like:

male friend   female guest   girl cousin.

I once saw a sign in a boys' hostel, which read:

Guests are allowed in members' rooms until midnight, unless they are female guests, in which case they are asked to leave by 10.30.

Usage gets a bit trickier when there isn't a 50–50 expectation about the sex referred to by the noun. Take these nouns:

doctor, chairman, engineer, nurse.

These days, even though the careers of such people are open to both sexes, there is still a long tradition favouring one sex, and this is reflected in modern usage. How else can you explain sentences such as the following:

They've a new lady doctor down at the surgery.

If the new arrival had been male, no one would have thought to say:

They've a new man doctor down at the surgery.

Whether you think this is right and proper, or scandalous, will depend on your attitude to the changing roles of women in society. Or the changing roles of men, in sentences like:

We've got a male nurse on our ward this week.

'Well, shall I be chairperson?'

Chairman is one of the words which has caused the most fuss, along with a few others ending in *-man*. Critics attacked these words early on in the feminist movement of the 1970s, because the words were felt to reflect the biases of a male-dominated society. They should be supplemented, or replaced, it was argued, by words more compatible with sexual equality. *Chairman* attracted special criticism, presumably because of the distinctive and influential social role involved in taking the chair at a meeting.

It's easy to pick on a word and kick it. Less easy to find an alternative that won't pose as many problems. Some people suggested *chairwoman* as a parallel to *chairman* – a word that's been used in English since the seventeenth century, in fact – but it didn't catch on. *Madam chairman* is the traditional mode of address for a woman in the chair, and is quite widely used in formal British English – but it didn't satisfy the demands for a properly neutral label.

The word which, in the end, came to be most used, especially in the U.S.A., was *chairperson*. It's nowadays very widely used in publicity for academic conferences, and the like, where the organizers (whether male or female) are aware of women participants who may feel offended by the use of *chairman*. On the other hand, the association of the new word with the extreme views of some feminists makes it a source of humour to many people. It still has only limited standing in the world of industry and commerce, where male domination evidently continues to be the norm.

Searching for new *-person* endings to English words makes an enjoyable pastime. Advertisements are a particularly fruitful field. Advertisers have had to devise ingenious ways of making sure that their ads don't cause offence, or break any laws. Often, the change is straightforward, as when *headteacher* is used in place of *headmaster*. *Salesman* is more awkward. Some ads say *salesman/saleswoman*. Others try to save space, and go for *salesperson*. But usage is mixed. The same applies to *spokesman*.

The tactics of extremists make it easy to joke about the whole issue of sexist language, which is a pity, for there are serious matters at stake. There's nothing funny about unequal status, unequal opportunity, unequal pay – and it's only natural to be concerned when there seems to be unequal language to talk about such things. So I don't laugh myself when I hear bad jokes like:

Did you hear about the feminist who wanted to write *history* as her-story!

But when you see the lengths people are prepared to go, to avoid sexist criticism of any kind, it's difficult to keep a straight face. I've seen *crafts-person*, *countryperson*, *postperson*, all in apparently serious contexts. And what do you think about the way in which some recent hymn books have had all sexist terms rigorously expurgated? 'Dear mother earth' became 'Earth ever fertile'. 'Mankind' became 'Humankind'. 'The brotherhood of man'? Out. 'God'? Can stay, if he/she is referred to neutrally. The result? More criticisms from the moderates than was ever received from the sexist extremists!

An interesting area of English usage is how we refer to inanimate objects, when we want to give them a personality. When we talk about a country as a political unit, for example, it is often referred to as feminine. We say:

England is proud of her history.

No one would think to say:

Germany had developed his economic growth . . .

When we refer affectionately to personal possessions, again the norm is feminine. I heard a stamp collector pick up a specimen and say:

Isn't she beautiful!

Cars are usually feminine, for both men and women – though I do know a woman who insists on referring to her sports car as *he*, and I know one man who called his car *Fred*, likewise referring to it by masculine pronouns only. Ships are generally feminine.

What about animate beings whose sex you don't know. Insects, for instance, whose sex only an expert could determine. They're mainly *it*, of course, especially if they have large numbers of legs. But if you're feeling at all affectionate towards them, then masculine pronouns are used.

Look at him, crawling along there,

said a father, talking to his child,

He's looking for some food . . .

The object in question was a cockroach.

Then there's the opposite situation. Human beings can be referred to as *it*, even when you do know what sex they are. A baby that cries in unsocial hours, for example! And examples like these. A sixteen-year-old girl, telling her friend about the previous evening's disco, said:

> Robert ignored me all evening, and then it finally asked me to dance!

A mother led her filthy five-year-old in from the garden, and said:

> Look at it! Have you ever seen such a mess!

At a party, a group of chatty friends contained one quiet member. The quiet one piped up after a while, somewhat unexpectedly, at which point one of the group commented:

> It spoke!

One of the most awkward usage problems arises when you don't want to say whether you're talking about a man or a woman. English doesn't easily let you do this. You can't use *it*, for that could be rude. *One* is a neutral form, but it is appropriate only for very formal situations or personalities, in speech. Many people avoid it, because it reminds them of the excessively formal speech style of some public figures, where

> One fell off one's horse

means 'I fell off my horse'. That leaves *he* or *she*. There isn't a nice, comfy, everyday neutral pronoun in English. Not when you're talking about just one person, anyway.

The problem comes to the boil in sentences beginning with a word like *anyone*, *anybody*, *someone* or *somebody*. Which pronoun would you put in the gap in this sentence?

> Anyone can have a drink if – wants.

The traditional usage here is *he* – which could be used even if women were part of the 'anyone'. But this has been attacked by feminists in recent years, an another example of the male bias of English.

What alternative is there? To replace by *she* wouldn't satisfy anyone. Males wouldn't use it. And females in any case would find it insulting, because of the nuance it can carry:

> Anyone can have a drink if she wants.

Of course, it would be possible to avoid the sexist lobby altogether, by using *he or she*, and this is what is usually done in formal writing

– either in full, or in an abbreviated form (writing *(s)he*, for instance). But it's a really awkward construction in speech:

Anyone can have a drink if he or she wants.

The informal way out of the problem has long been to use *they*, with a change of verb from singular to plural:

Anyone can have a drink if they want.

No problems with sex here! But unfortunately, this usage is like a red rag to a bull for traditional grammarians, who point to the singular sense of the word *anyone*, and say:

You can't have a plural *they* referring to a singular *anyone*!

But, needs must … And these days, *they* is in fact the commonest way out of the difficulty. It's even finding its way into contexts where it would never have appeared a generation ago without criticism. I've often heard it in questions in formal speech, for instance, where it passes unnoticed. Take this case, said by a school quizmaster:

Someone should be able to identify the author, shouldn't they?

Or this one, said by an M.P.:

Anybody might have found it, mightn't they?

So at present there are at least three usages competing for our attention, in such sentences: *he, he or she, they*. Several people have even invented a new pronoun, to get themselves out of the problem. I recall one proposal for *hem*, another for *shay*. What is *your* favourite way out?

Perhaps the most interesting example of a coinage which *has* caught on is *Ms*. It was originally suggested by feminists as a way out of the difficulty of classifying women in terms of their married status. Unlike *Master* and *Mr*, which are terms related to age, *Miss* and *Mrs* can both be used in adult life. 'Why should marriage be the distinguishing feature of a woman's title?' it was asked. The language needs a neutral term, like *Mr*.

Ms was suggested, to be used simply as a marker of 'Female', and saying nothing about her married state. It could therefore be used by anyone, whatever her status. And it came to be used by unmarried women, who didn't like *Miss*, by married women, who didn't like *Mrs*, and by others such as the following correspondent:

I like to be known as Ms. I have more experience than a Miss and I am no longer my husband's property, now that I am divorced. I feel it is important to be known and introduced as Ms, as it allows others to know my situation, rather than presume and be wrong.

Another female correspondent argued that:

Ms doesn't get round the problem of male domination, as long as women still take their father's name. Ms Smith, daughter of Mr Smith, is just as male as Mrs Brown, wife of Mr Brown. To be logical, a Ms ought to take her mother's name, before she was married.

A third says:

I've dropped titles altogether in letters, and use surname coupled with first name for formal occasions. Doing this for women leads quite naturally into doing it for men, too, so that gradually the identification of gender may fall into disuse.

This is quite a radical suggestion, for the written language – though it's on the increase in some fields, such as publishing or academic life. But it's not all that odd in speech, where people are often introduced to each other in this way, especially in professional circles:

Can I introduce Mary Jones?

Would you ever get:

Can I introduce Mrs Jones?

I think only if she were 'qualified' in some way, as:

Can I introduce Mrs Jones of our Accounts Department.

Or if she is known to be the wife of Mr Jones, to whom you've already been introduced.

It's obvious from the correspondence that women's feelings are mixed about Ms. Some use it. Some think it goes too far. Some think it doesn't go far enough. Men's feelings are mixed, too. Some dismiss it as an affectation. Some avoid it on principle, and I suppose would run the risk of being called male chauvinist pigs. But many men are finding it a useful strategy in writing, as it gives them a way out of the problem of how to address a woman whose status he is uncertain of. *Ms* these days even appears on some official forms, along with *Miss* and *Mrs*.

What about speech? *Ms* has had much less success in the spoken language, mainly due to uncertainty over its pronunciation. Is it 'miz' or 'muzz' or some kind of clipped 'mz'? 'Miz' seems to be winning, though it's often used in a self-conscious or jocular manner. It's perhaps too soon to say what is going to happen.

And now, ladies and gentlemen ...

When you're addressing a group of people, of both sexes, this would be the normal phrase to use. If they were all male, *gentlemen*. If they were all female, *ladies*. No problem.

But what if you wanted to single out just one person? And you don't know his/her name. You don't say:

Excuse me, gentleman.

Sir is the formal norm, which Americans use far more than the British. *Mister* is quite widespread, but that's informal. And there are several other possibilities, of various shades of informality and nuance. You might like to think which settings would be likely to bring forth the following, as terms of address. There's a space to make some notes.

Excuse me, man
         my lord.
         gaffer.
         my son.
         old chap.

Remember that some of these terms may have more than one type of setting. *Man*, for instance, might be used by hippies, Welshmen, Jamaicans ...

What about ladies?

Excuse me, lady.

Possible, in taxis, stations and other service areas – and especially in the U.S.A. But not appropriate for formal gatherings. *Madam* is widely used there. Miss is also quite polite. *Ms* hasn't yet achieved any standing. You don't hear:

Excuse me, Ms.

But you might hear any of the following. Once again, make a note of the setting where you might hear them:

Excuse me, girl.
        love.
        doll.
        my dear.
        milady.

Again, don't take things for granted, in an exercise of this kind. Take *darling*. If you're female and married, you may have had your husband use it to you. If you're female and walking along Portobello Road, you'll find it said to you, married or not. And sometimes if you're male, too, actually!

But what if you're talking about someone else, in his/her presence? Ladies first, this time. You're in the theatre, and someone points to a lady within earshot and asks:

Would you mind passing this programme to that — ?

What would you use? *Lady* seems to be the norm, these days. Many people would find *woman* abrupt or rude. The same applies to idiomatic phrases. *Young woman* isn't rude, but most people find it less courteous than *young lady*. And indeed, these days, *lady* seems to be replacing *woman* in other contexts too. If you're making an appreciative remark about someone, for instance, what would you say:

She's a very bright lady *or* ... woman?

Lady is on the increase, here. On the other hand, *woman* is often used as an adjective without any special implication:

She's a woman teacher

seems to mean the same as

She's a lady teacher.

Likewise,

She has a place in the women's finals

seems only slightly less formal than ... *ladies' finals*.

The *Spectator* ran a competition in April 1982. Competitors had to write a poem to define the word *lady*. The winning entry, by P. Carter, went as follows:

A Lady is a Woman
    who was a Lady

but now prefers
   to be a Woman
in order to distinguish her
   from the Lady
(who used to be a woman)
   who 'does' for her.

A further entry, by Joyce Johnson, gave a different slant:

A Lady with a large L
Is one who has to be
A born one or else wed to
The aristocracy.

A lady with a small l
Is one who keeps her place
By being very proper
And speaking very nace.

What about men? The problem isn't so serious. The theatre again:

Would you mind passing this programme to that — ?

pointing to a male. If the man were within earshot, you'd probably say
gentleman, to be polite. The same would apply in an office:

Would you ask this gentleman to wait outside

is courteous.

Would you ask this man to wait outside

isn't.

*

Ladies and gentlemen, boys and girls ... The list of sex-distinctive names
for people is a very long one. If you keep your ears open for them you
will find that they range from the conventional to the bizarre. On the
next page are some of the ones I've heard recently, in various contexts.
It shouldn't be difficult to add to the lists, and there's space to do so. Good
hunting!

Male	Female	Both
he-man	lass	darling
fellow	wench	chuck
guy	blonde	honey
bloke	mistress	love
beau	maiden	comrade
cove	spinster	
bachelor	doll	
mate	shrew	
johnny (He's a funny johnny, that one!)	female (If that female dares to come here, I'll …)	

Which is it? Round 4

31. She lives in a $\begin{Bmatrix} \text{luxurious} \\ \text{luxuriant} \end{Bmatrix}$ flat. _____

32. I've just $\begin{Bmatrix} \text{migrated} \\ \text{emigrated} \\ \text{immigrated} \end{Bmatrix}$ from England. _____

33. The findings $\begin{Bmatrix} \text{militate} \\ \text{mitigate} \end{Bmatrix}$ against the view that he's innocent. _____

34. John is a very $\begin{Bmatrix} \text{practical} \\ \text{practicable} \end{Bmatrix}$ person. _____

35. A doctor $\begin{Bmatrix} \text{prescribes} \\ \text{proscribes} \end{Bmatrix}$ medicine. _____

36. He's the $\begin{Bmatrix} \text{principle} \\ \text{principal} \end{Bmatrix}$ violinist. _____

37. His $\begin{Bmatrix} \text{prophecy} \\ \text{prophesy} \end{Bmatrix}$ has come true. _____

38. I $\begin{Bmatrix} \text{refute} \\ \text{deny} \end{Bmatrix}$ that ludicrous accusation. _____

39. You're trying to $\begin{Bmatrix} \text{sew} \\ \text{sow} \end{Bmatrix}$ some doubts in my mind. _____

40. I'm going to buy some more $\begin{Bmatrix} \text{stationary} \\ \text{stationery} \end{Bmatrix}$. _____

(*Solutions are on p. 123*)

Eternal tolerance

> The condition upon which God hath given liberty to man is eternal vigilance.

So said John Philpot Curran, the champion of Irish liberties, in a speech in 1790. 'Eternal vigilance' is a phrase many people have adopted, as part of their approach to the English language. Only by being continually on the alert, they say, can the language be safeguarded from decline. Some go further, and form societies to protect the language from abuse. Letters to the BBC regularly ask for a clean-up campaign. One letter I received wanted the language 'disinfected'. Another, using a metaphor whose implications I still ponder, wanted it 'sterilized'!

It's a linguistic fact of life that everyone has a set of likes and dislikes about other people's usage – self included. And, as we've seen, many people are ready to take up the linguistic equivalent of a butterfly net, and go out hunting for prize specimens of what they see as language abuse. Several people collect intrusive *r*s, it seems, found mainly in the winding valleys of Radio 2, if my correspondence is to be believed. Others collect split infinitives – great herds of them on Radio 1, I've been told. One correspondent offered me selections of misplaced prepositions, which – if I understood his letter correctly – he thought of as a stamp collection, for he offered to swap some of his for some of mine.

Now there's no harm, and there can be a great deal of fun, in collecting bits of language that you like and dislike. Some people have even made a living out of it. But there's a trap. The exercise can quickly turn sour, if you approach it in a negative, bitchy frame of mind. There's a world of difference between:

> I don't like the way John Smith talks

and:

> I don't like the way John Smith talks, and I'm jolly well going to do something about it

– by starting up a campaign of public ridicule and condemnation. People get hurt, when this happens. There are cases on record of people losing their jobs because their employer didn't like the way they spoke. The hurt can go deeper. The *Daily Express* ran a story a few years ago, which began:

> Blacksmith X died a victim of dialect snobbery. He killed himself at 70 because he was ashamed of his Yorkshire accent when he went to live in the South, it was said at the inquest . . .

The consequences of our linguistic intolerance are indeed hard to foresee.

But what if the clean-up campaign isn't focused on any one person? What if your attitude is:

> I don't like the way *most* people talk,

or even:

> I don't like the way anyone talks – including me!

in relation to some particular point of usage. The over-use of *you know*, for instance. Or putting stress on the wrong syllable. Correspondents, in criticizing others, often blame themselves too. In fact, the most common metaphor used in letters about usage is a religious one. People talk about 'committing sins' of usage themselves, and of 'confessing' their errors. One correspondent went so far as to ask me – of all people – for absolution! Now, if they are serious, is this not a different kind of trap – the trap of wasted emotional energy, that might have been more fruitfully spent on other aspects of living? For no matter how they try, they cannot stop the tide (as King Canute might say) of usage.

'But you can! You can!' it's sometimes said in reply. 'If enough people shout . . .' 'If enough of us give a lead . . .' '*Someone* must be concerned about falling standards these days . . .' Yes, of course. If standards *are* falling, then there's cause for concern, and people should shout. If speakers and writers are unclear, ambiguous, unintelligible, confused, something ought to be done. But are the usage issues discussed in this book cases of this kind? And are things worse today than ever before?

I'll take the second question first, because the answer is easy. No. Or, if you want it put more circumspectly: there's no evidence that linguistic standards are worse today then they were, say, a hundred years ago. Consider this quotation, for instance:

> A correspondent asks me to notice a usage now becoming prevalent among persons who ought to know better, viz. that of 'you and I' after prepositions governing the accusative.

Or this one:

> Look, to take one familiar example, at the process of deterioration
> which our Queen's English has undergone at the hands of the
> Americans. Look at those phrases which so amuse us in their speech
> and books; at their reckless exaggeration, and contempt for
> congruity ...

These are no letters to the BBC – though they might have been. They
are taken from Henry Alford's *The Queen's English*, published in the 1860s.
And almost every usage issue discussed in my book can be found in
his – or in even earlier grammars and manuals of the eighteenth and
nineteenth centuries. It's easy to think that usage problems are new,
or recent – that standards are deteriorating *now*, and that someone or
something must be to blame. And if you want a scapegoat, you'll find
one, lurking in the corridors of the BBC, or the national press. But things
haven't really changed much in the past hundred years.

What has changed, of course, is our *awareness* of usage variation.
That's been the main effect of radio, television, the press, and the media
explosion in general – to keep before our eyes and ears the existence
of language variety. We see and hear more language than ever before.
In a single listening or viewing day, we encounter a host of Englishes,
belonging to people of all kinds of regional and social backgrounds. They
clamour for our attention, and we have to react to them. They force
us to question our own identities, our loyalties, our tastes. In the old
days, people weren't exposed to so many pressures. What the ear didn't
hear, the heart didn't grieve about. These days, we hear and see so
much, we can't help but grieve, some of the time.

So to return to my other question. Are the usage issues in this book
worth getting upset about? Yes and no. Some of the issues seem to lead
nowhere. If, by some magic, everyone were to stop using split infinitives
tomorrow, what actually would have been achieved? My argument is:
Nothing – and something might even have been lost. Several issues in
this book suggest this kind of conclusion. On the other hand, certain
usage topics have brought to light real problems of a linguistic or social
kind, where unthinking language can lead to misunderstanding,
disaccord, open hostility. These matters are certainly worth getting upset
about, for they affect the way we live – not just the way we write and
teach our grammars.

My aim in writing this book has been to help you develop a sense
of priorities, when faced with usage problems. Some problems are really

quite minor. Others are very serious. If you go around thinking that English usage doesn't matter at all – that 'anything goes' – you'll quickly get into trouble. Likewise, if you go around thinking that the whole of English usage is a minefield – that 'nothing goes'. The reality is in between. What's needed is the exchange of new linguistic lamps for old – lamps which will show the colours of modern English to be not just black and white, right *vs* wrong, but many shades of grey and cream. You don't lose your sense of standards by doing this. On the contrary, seeing the contrasts in colour is certain to improve your linguistic sensitivity.

But the lamp-exchange will take a while. You can't climb out of the straitjacket of two hundred years of grammatical tradition overnight. It's a slow process, which starts with books of this kind. Whether you agree with my observations about English usage or not, I hope they have made you reflect about what is going on. I hope you are now more ready to question the linguistic prescriptions you may have learned in childhood – to see whether they really work. I hope you will feel like finding out more about the history and variety of English – not just by collecting facts, but by trying to establish the reasons for the way things are. My approach doesn't ask you to stop being vigilant, as speaker and listener, reader and writer – but it does ask you to be considerate, while you're on watch. It asks you to care, as well as to take care. Eternal vigilance? Certainly. But in a civilized society, eternal tolerance, too.

Something to read?

If you want to read more about English usage, there's no shortage of choice. I would begin with Randolph Quirk's *The Use of English* (Longman, 2nd edn, 1968). Then there's Brian Foster's *The Changing English Language* (Penguin Books, 1970) or Charles Barber's *Linguistic Change in Present-Day English* (Oliver & Boyd, 1964). A convenient collection of readings about the language, from 1858 to the present day, is in *The English Language*, Vol. 2, edited by Whitney Bolton and myself (C.U.P., 1969). Bolton also edited Vol. 10 of the Sphere History of Literature in the English Language, which was devoted to the language alone: *The English Language* (Sphere Books, 1975). Many aspects of English, ancient and modern, are dealt with in the Blackwell/Deutsch *Language Library*, which now contains over fifty volumes, representing both traditional and linguistic attitudes to language. If you are unfamiliar with the usage manuals which set the linguistic tone in the early part of this century, then you should look at one or other of them: perhaps H. W. and F. G. Fowler, *The King's English* (O.U.P., 1906), or Sir Ernest Gowers' *The Complete Plain Words* (H.M.S.O., 1954), or Eric Partridge's *Usage and Abusage* (Penguin Books, 1963). An interesting modern study, which uses a questionnaire technique to find out about current opinions, is W. H. Mittins and others, *Attitudes to English Usage* (O.U.P., 1970). A recent guide to regional varieties of standard English is Peter Trudgill & Jean Hannah, *International English* (Edward Arnold, 1982). A fascinating collection of articles on the subject is to be found in Leonard Michaels and Christopher Ricks, *The State of the Language* (University of California Press, 1980).

Next please

This book contains only some of the problems of English usage that people talk about. If I've missed one of the topics which interest you, and you'd like to see it included in a further book of Who cares ...? then use this page. Send in any suggestions to: the author, c/o Penguin Books Ltd, 536 King's Road, London SW10 0UH.

Solutions to Which is it?

1. ACCEPT is correct. The two words have the same pronunciation in everyday speech, and this often leads to spelling confusion. There is no overlap in their meaning. *Except* means 'leave out', 'exclude', etc., as in *Everyone must come. No one is excepted. Accept* has the meaning 'take in', 'admit', etc., as in the test sentence. *Except* may also be used as a preposition, as in *They all passed the exam except Mike.*

2. AFFECTED is correct. Another pair of words whose similar pronunciation in normal speech causes frequent spelling confusion. It's important to note that *affect* is most widely used as a verb, in its meanings of 'cause to change' or 'arouse feelings', as in the test sentence. *Affect*, as a noun, is little used outside of psychology: when psychologists study *affect*, they are looking at the emotional side of behaviour. By contrast, *effect* is most widely used as a noun, with such meanings as 'result', as in *Look at the effect of that rain on the garden!* Its use as a verb, meaning 'cause', is uncommon, and restricted to formal situations.

3. ILLUSIONS is correct. Another case of similar pronunciations causing problems. *Allusion* means 'indirect reference', as in *He made no allusion to the danger. Illusion* means 'unreal or false perception or belief', as in the test sentence.

4. AMENDED is correct. More similar pronunciations. *Emend* is a word which has a very restricted meaning – 'to edit or change a piece of text'. *Amend* is much more general in its meaning of 'change, improve', as in the test sentence.

5. ENSURE is correct. At least in British English. American English often uses *insure* in this context, and it has a limited British usage. But usually *insure* is more specific, in British English, as it refers just to the area of financial protection through 'insurance', whereas *ensure* has a much broader sense of 'make certain'. *Assure* means 'promise, persuade', etc., and applies to persons, as in *I assure you it won't happen again.*

6. BEREFT is correct. The sense required is one of general deprivation. Only in the context of loss due to death would *bereaved* be appropriate.

7. BIANNUAL is correct. Both words are fairly uncommon, and their similar construction leads to problems. *Biannual* means 'twice a year'. *Biennial* means 'once in two years'.

8. BORNE is correct. This is the spelling to use when the sense is 'carry', etc., as in the test sentence. If the meaning were 'give birth to', both spellings are used, as in *He was born in Reading* and *Two children were borne to her while she lived in America*.

9. CEREMONIAL is correct. This adjective refers to ceremony in general, and is the appropriate term to use when talking about occasions, types of dress, and so on. It applies only to things or events. *Ceremonious* applies to the behaviour of people, whenever they act in a formal or pompous way, as in *He walked ceremoniously out of the room*.

10. CLASSIC is correct. The sense required is 'typical, excellent'. *Classical* has a more restricted meaning, referring to historical origins, and especially to ancient Greek or Roman culture.

Round 2

11. COMPLIMENTARY is correct. The two pronunciations are the same, so spellings are often confused. *Compliment(ary)* is the one to use when expression of praise is involved; *complement(ary)* when the sense is to do with completion, as in *Their interests are complementary, rather than competitive*.

12. CONTEMPTIBLE is correct. The difference between these two words is to do with the direction of the criticism. Who is affected by the contempt? If I make a *contemptuous* comment about someone, it is he who receives the force of my contempt. But if I make a *contemptible* comment about someone, it is other people who will feel contempt for me.

13. COUNCIL is correct. Again, identical pronunciations lead to spelling confusion. *Council* refers to the group of people, each of whom is a *councillor*. They shouldn't be confused with people who give general advice: they are *counsellors*, and what they give is *counsel*. *Counsel* can also be used as a verb: *He counselled me about the move . . . Council* can't.

14. CREDIBLE is correct. *Credible* means 'trustworthy, deserving of belief'. *Credulous* refers to someone who is too ready to believe anything, especially without good reason: *John's a very credulous individual*.

15. DEFINITELY is correct. This is the usual word to use when the meaning is simply one of certainty. *Definitive* refers to something that can't be questioned or improved, as in a *definitive account of what happened*.

16. DEPRECATE is correct. This is a somewhat formal word, meaning

'express disapproval'. *Depreciate* is used when the meaning is 'lessen in value', as in *He's always depreciated my achievements*. These days, *deprecate* will often be heard in this second sense also, but the usage is often criticized.

17. DISTINCT is correct. The meaning required is 'clear, plain'. *Distinctive* has the meaning 'marking something as different', as in *She wore a distinctive dress*.

18. ECONOMIC is correct. This is the word to use when you are talking about the field of economics. *Economical* is used when you are talking about not being wasteful: *I've got a very economical car*. You sometimes see advertisements using *economic* in the latter sense (*It has to be an economic proposition*, said one), but this usage isn't widespread – yet.

19. ELECTRICAL is correct. *Electric* lights, drills, chairs ... this is the form to use when you're referring to an implement that produces electricity or is powered by it. *Electrical* faults, connections, engineers ... this is the form to use when you're talking generally about the subject of electricity or its people.

20. EMINENT is correct. Happenings are *imminent* – they are about to take place. People are *eminent* – famous, outstanding.

Round 3

21. EXCEPTIONAL is correct. The person's intellect is really unusual or remarkable. *Exceptionable* applies to something which is a source of objection, as in *I can't see anything exceptionable in that programme*.

22. NON-FLAMMABLE is correct. The context makes it clear that the material won't burn. *Inflammable* is often misunderstood, because people think the *in-* means 'not' (as it does in *visible–invisible*). In fact, its job is simply to intensify the meaning of *flammable* – as in the verb *inflame* (which doesn't mean to extinguish!). These days, people are aware of the ambiguity, and *flammable* seems to be replacing *inflammable* as the general word of warning.

23. FLOUTING is correct. *Flout* means 'treat without respect'. *Flaunt* means 'show something off'. Rules and regulations are often flouted. Cars, clothes and other possessions are often flaunted. You'll often hear *flaunt* being used in place of *flout*, these days, but it's a usage which has no status in standard English as yet.

24. FORTUITOUS is correct. The context makes it clear that the remark couldn't be *fortunate*: you don't regret something that's lucky. *Fortuitous*

means 'accidental'. In a context such as 'What a — meeting!' either could be used, depending on what was meant.

25. HISTORIC is correct. The word *now* disallows *historical*, which is the appropriate term to use when you're talking about events in the past, or about history in general. A *historical play* is one about things that once took place. *Historic* has the more general sense of 'important' – either in the past or in the present. *That was a historic day for England* illustrates the past usage. The test sentence illustrates the present.

26. IMPLIED is correct. It is the speaker or writer who *implies* – that is, 'suggests' or 'hints'. It is the listener or reader who *infers* – that is, 'draws a conclusion'. *Infer* is often loosely used in the first sense, but the usage has no formal status in standard English.

27. AFFLICTED is correct. The meanings of the two words are similar, but the usage is quite different. Someone is *afflicted with* suffering or trouble, as in the test sentence. Something unpleasant is *inflicted on* (or *upon*) a person, as in *Don't you dare inflict that child on me!*

28. INGENIOUS is correct. *Ingenuous* is said of people and their actions – referring to their naïve simplicity. *You do know what they're up to. Don't be ingenuous!*, someone might say. *Ingenious* means 'clever, intricate', and can refer to things as well as people.

29. LICENCE is correct. In Britain, that is. British English makes a distinction between the noun *licence* and the verb *to license*. In American English, *license* is used for both.

30. LIGHTNING is correct. At normal conversational speed, the pronunciations are the same, hence they are often confused in spelling. *Lightning* is the noun which goes with thunder. *Lightening* is from the verb *lighten*: *He is lightening his load.*

Round 4

31. LUXURIOUS is correct. Unless, that is, the flat were so full of growing things, that it was beginning to resemble a jungle! *Luxuriant* is the word to use in the context of 'growth'. *Luxurious* relates to physical comfort, especially your surroundings or way of living. These days, *luxury* is often used instead of *luxurious*, in such phrases as *luxury goods*, *luxury tours*.

32. EMIGRATED is correct. Animals and birds, as well as people, *migrate*, and when they do so, they usually come back a season later. *Emigrate* and *immigrate* are used only of people, who make a once-and-for-all move. You usually emigrate *from* somewhere – though these days, the verb

is often used with *to*, as in *He's finally emigrated to Australia.* You usually immigrate *to* somewhere – but this usage is much less common.

33. MILITATE is correct. *Militate against* is a phrase which means 'serves as a reason against', as in the test sentence. *Mitigate* means 'lessen the seriousness of' something: *He tried to mitigate the harm he'd done by apologizing.* In recent years, *mitigate* has often come to be used in place of *militate*, but this is not an acceptable standard usage, and attracts a great deal of criticism.

34. PRACTICAL is correct. *Practicable* is not used about people: it refers to something that can be successfully used, as in *Is it practicable to travel by road? Practical* can refer to people, implying their efficiency or sensibleness, as in the test sentence. When it refers to things, it stresses actual conditions rather than possible ideas – what is now, not what might be. So you can have both a *practical idea*, which should work straight away, and a *practicable idea*, which might work in the future.

35. PRESCRIBES is correct. This word applies to something that can or should be done. *Proscribe* applies to things that should not be done, as when a grammar book proscribes a particular usage – it forbids it.

36. PRINCIPAL is correct. The two words sound the same, so their spelling is often confused. Only *principal* can act as an adjective, as in the test sentence. As a noun, it means 'chief'. *Principle*, as a noun, has an abstract meaning – a truth or belief – as in *I respect his principles.*

37. PROPHECY is correct. Same pronunciation, but an important grammatical difference. *Prophecy* is the noun. *Prophesy* is the verb, as in *I prophesy that he will survive.*

38. DENY is correct. If someone accuses you, all that you can do as an immediate reaction is deny it. If you want to *refute* what someone has said, then you must gather evidence together, and argue the point: *I shall have no difficulty in refuting your argument.* In recent years, *refute* has begun to be used in the sense of *deny*. Trades union speakers, for example, are often heard 'refuting' the slanderous attacks of management. But this usage continues to be criticized as non-standard.

39. SOW is correct. You *sow* seeds, doubts, uncertainty. You *sew* buttons, clothes, leather.

40. STATIONERY is correct. Identical pronunciations again. This is the word to use for the writing materials. *Stationary* for lack of movement.

Penguin Reference Books

ROGET'S THESAURUS

Edited and specially adapted for this edition by Susan Lloyd

The first revision for twenty years – reflecting recent changes in spoken and written English.

Specially adapted for Penguins, this latest version is in direct line of descent from Roget's original. Now updated to include new concepts like data processing, hatchback, mole and sitcom, and still ranging from literary to the colloquial, the scientific to the philosophical, *Roget's Thesaurus* is an invaluable work of reference – it is indeed a 'treasure house' of words!

'As normal a part of an intelligent household's library as the Bible, Shakespeare and a dictionary' – *Daily Telegraph*

'That hardy standby of authors, translators, advertising copywriters, crossword-solvers and indeed any of us with an interest in words' – *Sunday Times Magazine*

'Ms Lloyd has now improved it, with more new locutions and a touch of feminism' – *Sunday Telegraph*

'An established classic among works of reference' – *The Times Educational Supplement*

THE PENGUIN DICTIONARY OF TROUBLESOME WORDS

Bill Bryson

Why should you avoid discussing the *weather conditions?*

Can a married woman be *celibate?*

Why is it eccentric to talk about the *aroma* of a cowshed?

Can you identify a *non sequitur*, a *split compound verb*, or a *dangling modifier?*

This dictionary provides a straightforward guide to the pitfalls and hotly disputed issues in standard written English. The entries are discussed with wit and commonsense, and illustrated with examples of questionable usages taken from leading British and American newspapers, plus occasional references to masters of the language such as Samuel Johnson and Shakespeare.

No familiarity with English grammar is needed to learn from this book, although a glossary of grammatical terms is included and there is also an appendix on punctuation. Journalists, copy-writers and secretaries will find this an invaluable handbook, as will crossword buffs and everyone else involved with the written word, whether for business or pleasure.

Penguin Reference Books

THE PENGUIN DICTIONARY OF
HISTORICAL SLANG

Eric Partridge

abridged by Jacqueline Simpson

This volume has been the standard work on the subject for years – now Penguin have extracted the most valuable parts of it, including all the expressions coined or used before 1914, to make up the present 50,000 entries.

Often wry and flippant, occasionally 'blue', and sometimes uproariously funny, they recapture the rich idiom of English life and language through the ages, recalling the vigour of Elizabethan phrase, the ribald tongue of dockside and pub, the richer coinages of messdeck and barracks, the euphemisms and witticisms of the nineteenth-century drawing room, and the irrepressible wit of errand boys and costermongers.